The MCP *Literature*
P R O G R A M

C

Marjorie Slavick Frank
Creative Writer, Linguist, Teacher

P. J. Hutchins
Supervisor, Bureau of Reading
Education, New York State Education
Department, New York City Regional Office

Project Design and Supervision: The Quarasan Group, Inc.
Project Editor: Craig Strasshofer
Text Research: Diane Person, Librarian, Polytechnic Preparatory
   Country Day School, Brooklyn, NY

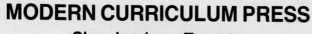
MODERN CURRICULUM PRESS
Cleveland • Toronto

Acknowledgements: 1. This text edition of THE KOMODO DRAGON'S JEWELS by D. R. Massey, is reprinted by arrangement with Macmillan Publishing Company. 2. Specified illustrations and text of WHO'S A PEST by Crosby Newell Bonsall. Copyright © 1962 by Crosby Newell Bonsall. Reprinted by permission of Harper & Row, Publishers Inc. 3. "The Centipede" from THE SHERIFF OF ROTTENSHOT by Jack Prelutsky, copyright © 1982 by Jack Prelutsky, used by permission of Greenwillow Books (a division of William Morrow & Co.). 4. "Sea Song" from AROUND AND ABOUT by Marchette Chute, copyright © 1957, reprinted by permission of the author. 5. "Mitzi Takes A Taxi" from TELL ME A MITZI by Lore Segal, with pictures by Harriet Pincus. Text copyright © 1970 by Lore Segal. Reprinted by permission of Farrar, Straus & Giroux, Inc. 6. "The Browns Take the Day Off" text of pages 9–15 from THERE IS A CARROT IN MY EAR AND OTHER NOODLE TALES retold by Alvin Schwartz. Text copyright © 1982 by Alvin Schwartz. Reprinted by permission of Harper & Row, Publishers Inc. 7. MIGUEL'S MOUNTAIN by Bill Binzen, copyright © 1968 by Bill Binzen, reprinted by permission of Coward, McCann & Geoghegan, Inc. 8. "The Sun and the Wind" by Sally Jarvis IN LITTLE PLAYS FOR LITTLE PEOPLE, copyright © 1965 by Parent's Magazine Press, Reprinted by permission of Four Winds Press, a division of Scholastic, Inc. 9. "Which Piece is Mine?" by Barbara Walker from LITTLE PLAYS FOR LITTLE PEOPLE, copyright © 1965 by Parent's Magazine Press. Reprinted by permission of Scholastic, Inc. 10. Chapter 5 of THE SOD HOUSE by Elizabeth Coatsworth, copyright © 1954, is reprinted by arrangement with Macmillan Publishing Company. 11. "Eletelephony" by Laura E. Richards, copyright © 1932 by Laura E. Richards, copyright renewed © 1960 by Hamilton Richards. Reprinted by permission of Little, Brown and Company. 12. "The Six Wise Travelers" by Sally Jarvis from LITTLE PLAYS FOR LITTLE PEOPLE, copyright © 1965 by Parent's Magazine Press. Reprinted by permission of Four Winds Press, a division of Scholastic Inc. 13. THE MAGIC FISH by Freya Littledale. Text copyright © 1967 by Freya Littledale. Reprinted by permission of Scholastic Inc. 14. "The Monkey's Heart" by Eleanor B. Heady from SAFIRI THE SINGER AND OTHER TALES copyright © 1970 by Eleanor B. Heady. Reprinted by permission of Modern Curriculum Press, Inc. 15. "The Gingerbread Man" from THE DAY IS DANCING by Rowena Bennett, copyright © 1968 by Rowena Bastin Bennett. Reprinted by permission of Modern Curriculum Press, Inc. 16. "Prickled Pickles Don't Smile" by Nikki Giovanni from VACATION TIME copyright © 1980 by Nikki Giovanni. Reprinted by permission of William Morrow & Co. 17. "The First Day of School" from RAMONA QUIMBY, AGE 8 by Beverly Cleary, copyright © 1981 by Beverly Cleary. Reprinted by permission of William Morrow & Co. 18. ALEXANDRA THE ROCK EATER by Dorothy Van Woerkom. Copyright © 1978 by Dorothy Van Woerkom. Reprinted by permission of Alfred A. Knopf, Inc. 19. "The Bird of Seven Colors" from THE THREE WISHES by Ricardo Alegria, copyright © 1969 by Ricardo Alegria. Reprinted by permission of the author. 20. "Keep a Poem in Your Pocket" from SOMETHING SPECIAL by Beatrice Schenk de Regniers, copyright © 1958, 1968 by Beatrice Schenk de Regniers. Reprinted by permission of the author. 21. "School is Over' from UNDER THE WINDOW by Kate Greenaway. Reprinted by permission of Frederick Warnes & Company. 22. "Poem" from THE DREAMKEEPER AND OTHER POEMS by Langston Hughes. Copyright © 1932 by Alfred A. Knopf, Inc., renewed 1960 by Langston Hughes. Reprinted by permission of Alfred A. Knopf, Inc. 23. "Cats" by Eleanor Farjeon, copyright © 1957 by Eleanor Farjeon. Reprinted by permission of Harold Ober Associates Inc. 24. "The Little Rain" from FLASHLIGHT AND OTHER POEMS by Judith Thurman, copyright © 1976 by Judith Thurman. Reprinted with the permission of Atheneum Publishers. 25. "Skinned Knee" from FLASHLIGHT AND OTHER POEMS by Judith Thurman, copyright © 1976 by Judith Thurman. Reprinted with the permission of Atheneum Publishers. 26. "STAND BACK," SAID THE ELEPHANT, "I'M GOING TO SNEEZE" by Patricia Thomas, copyright © 1971 by Patricia Thomas. Reprinted by permission of Lothrop, Lee & Shepard Books (a division of William Morrow & Company). 27. From SANTIAGO by Pura Belpré, copyright © 1969 by Pura Belpré. Reprinted by permission of Viking Penguin Inc. 28. KEVIN'S GRANDMA by Barbara Williams, illustrated by Kay Chorao. Text copyright © 1975 by Barbara Williams. Reprinted by permission of the publisher, E. P. Dutton, a division of New American Library.

Every reasonable effort has been made to locate the ownership of copyrighted materials and to make due acknowledgement. Any errors or omissions will gladly be rectified in future editions.

Illustration credits: The Komodo Dragon's Jewels, Toni Hormann; Skill Focus p. 17, Rick Incrocci; Who's A Pest, Crosby Newell Bonsall; The Centipede, John Hayes; Sea Song, Kurt Mitchell; Mitzi Takes A Taxi, Joe Van Severen; The Browns Take the Day Off, Michael Streff; Genre Focus p. 41, Joe Van Severen; Miguel's Mountain, Janice Skivington Wood; The Sun and the Wind, Paul Turnbaugh; Genre Focus p. 57, Rick Incrocci; Which Piece is Mine?, Toni Hormann; The Sod House, Joe Van Severen; Eletelephony, John Hayes; As I Was Going Out One Day, George Suyeoka; The Six Wise Travelers, Toni Hormann; Skill Focus p. 74–75, Joe Van Severen; The Magic Fish, Paul Turnbaugh; The Monkey's Heart, George Suyeoka; Genre Focus p. 88, George Suyeoka; The Gingerbread Man, Toni Hormann; Prickled Pickles Don't Smile, Joe Develasco; The First Day of School, Janice Skivington Wood; Alexandra the Rock-Eater, Paul Turnbaugh; Skill Focus p. 119, Rick Incrocci; The Bird of Seven Colors, George Suyeoka; Keep a Poem in Your Pocket, Joe Van Severen; School is Over, Paul Turnbaugh; Poem, Joe Van Severen; Cats, Larry Frederick; Skill Focus p. 134, Lynn Biron; The Little Rain, Toni Hormann; Skinned Knee, Janice Skivington Wood; "Stand Back," Said the Elephant, "I Think I'm Going to Sneeze", Michael Streff; Santiago, Joe Van Severen; Kevin's Grandma, Michael Streff

ISBN 0-8136-1803-7   2 3 4 5 6 7 8 9   90 89 88 87

Table of Contents

Unit 1   SURPRISES   page 5

The Komodo Dragon's Jewels
by Diane Redfield Massey 6
 ■ Talk, Think, Write 15

SKILL FOCUS
Understanding Plot 16

Who's A Pest?
by Crosby Newell Bonsall 18
 ■ Talk, Think, Write 27

Spotlight on Crosby Newell Bonsall 28

The Centipede
by Jack Prelutsky 29

Sea Song
by Marchette Chute 30

Mitzi Takes A Taxi
by Lore Segal 32
 ■ Talk, Think, Write 38

The Browns Take the Day Off
by Alvin Schwartz 39
 ■ Talk, Think, Write 40

GENRE FOCUS
Enjoying Fiction 41

Miguel's Mountain
by Bill Binzen 42
 ■ Talk, Think, Write 51

At The Library 52

Unit 2   TROUBLES   page 53

The Sun and the Wind
by Sally Jarvis 54
 ■ Talk, Think, Write 56

GENRE FOCUS
Enjoying Plays 57

Which Piece is Mine?
by Barbara Walker 58
 ■ Talk, Think, Write 60

The Sod House
by Elizabeth Coatsworth 61
 ■ Talk, Think, Write 66

Spotlight on Elizabeth Coatsworth 67

Eletelephony
by Laura E. Richards 68

As I Was Going Out One Day
anonymous 69

The Six Wise Travelers
by Sally Jarvis 70
 ■ Talk, Think, Write 73

SKILL FOCUS
Understanding Setting 74

The Magic Fish
by Freya Littledale 76
 ■ Talk, Think, Write 81

At The Library 82

Unit 3 TRICKS   page 83

The Monkey's Heart
by Eleanor B. Heady 84
■ Talk, Think, Write 87

GENRE FOCUS
Enjoying Folk Literature 88

The Gingerbread Man
by Rowena Bennett 89

Prickled Pickles Don't Smile
by Nikki Giovanni 90

The First Day of School
by Beverly Cleary 91
■ Talk, Think, Write 102

Spotlight on Beverly Cleary 103

Alexandra the Rock-Eater
by Dorothy Van Woerkom 104
■ Talk, Think, Write 117

SKILL FOCUS
Understanding Characters 118

The Bird of Seven Colors
by Ricardo Alegria 120
■ Talk, Think, Write 125

At The Library 126

Unit 4 FRIENDSHIP page 127

Keep a Poem in Your Pocket
by Beatrice Schenk de Regniers 128

GENRE FOCUS
Enjoying Poetry 129

School is Over
by Kate Greenaway 130

Poem
by Langston Hughes 131

Spotlight on Langston Hughes 132

Cats
by Eleanor Farjeon 133

SKILL FOCUS
Understanding Shape Poetry 134

The Little Rain
by Judith Thurman 135

Skinned Knee
by Judith Thurman 136

"Stand Back," Said the Elephant, "I'm Going To Sneeze"
by Patricia Thomas 137
■ Talk, Think, Write 142

Santiago
by Pura Belpré 143
■ Talk, Think, Write 155

Kevin's Grandma
by Barbara Williams..................... 156
■ Talk, Think, Write 159

At The Library............................. 160

Surprises

What happens when a lizard decides to take a boat ride?

How can a pest turn out to be a hero?

What kind of taxi ride goes nowhere?

How can a mountain appear suddenly in the middle of a city?

There are lots of surprises in store for the story characters in this unit—and a few just for you.

Some tourists are vacationing on board a ship. They stop to explore an island. As they wander around the tiny spot of land, they set the stage for the biggest surprise of their lives.

The Komodo Dragon's Jewels

by DIANE REDFIELD MASSIE

The Komodo Dragon was a great green lizard. He lived by himself on an island in the sea. On clear nights he could see the lights from the mainland. He thought they were jewels.

"That must be a beautiful place," said the Komodo Dragon to himself. "Someday I'll go to see those jewels."

One day a ship sailed into the bay.

"What a beautiful island!" said the tourists on board. "Let's visit it!"

---

island (EYE-lund) land with water all around it

tourists (TOO-rists) people who travel for fun

6

They came ashore in rowboats and wandered over the island.

"It's as green as a jewel!" said Miss Mildew, who was one of the passengers. "I'm going to pick flowers."

Miss Mildew's big green hat matched her long green gown, and soon she was lost among the vines.

"All aboard!" called the Captain from the ship.

The tourists ran over the rocks and climbed into the rowboats. (All but Miss Mildew—she was picking trumpet flowers.)

"Miss Mildew," called the others. "It's time to go back to the ship!"

"What?" said the Komodo Dragon, waking up from his nap. "Time to go to the ship?"

He rubbed his eyes and crawled slowly over the rocks toward the boats.

"Miss Mildew! Miss Mildew!" called the tourists. "There she is, crawling over the rocks! Hurry, Miss Mildew," they said.

They rowed back to the ship, leaving a boat for Miss Mildew on the beach.

"They've left me a boat!" said the Komodo Dragon. "How very kind. I'll join them and go to see the jewels on the mainland!"

He climbed into the rowboat and rowed himself out to the ship. Then he crawled aboard

---

trumpet (TRUM-pet) bell-shaped, like the end of the musical instrument

and sat down in a deck chair. The ship blew its whistle, and off they sailed toward the mainland.

"Would you like some iced tea?" asked a waiter, looking out the door.

"Thank you," said the Komodo Dragon, "That would be very nice."

The waiter went back to the galley.

"Miss Mildew would like iced tea," he said. "And she looks more like a lizard than ever."

He carried the tea outside.

The Komodo Dragon smiled, showing his big green teeth.

"Thank you," he said.

"HELP!" cried the waiter. "IT *IS* A LIZARD!" And he ran inside.

"Of course I'm a lizard," said the Komodo Dragon to himself. "That's nothing to get excited about."

galley (GAH-lee) the kitchen on a ship or boat

He sipped his tea slowly from a straw and watched the blue-green sea. The tourists inside said, "Nonsense! A big lizard in a deck chair! How absurd!"

Dong! Dong! Dong! rang the dinner bell. The tourists went into the dining room. They sat in their usual places.

"Miss Mildew will sit at the Captain's table tonight," announced the headwaiter.

"Lucky Miss Mildew!" said everyone.

The waiters served the food.

"I'm hungry," said the Komodo Dragon. He stretched his green legs and stood up. "And I smell food."

He went inside. Soon he found the dining room door and opened it.

"There's Miss Mildew," whispered the tourists.

"Your chair is next to the Captain," said the waiter, carrying the bread.

The Komodo Dragon sat down on the Captain's right.

absurd (ub-SURD) very silly, foolish

"Lovely evening," said the Captain, staring at his soup.

"Lovely," said the Komodo Dragon.

He tied his napkin under his chin and drank his soup in one gulp.

"How soon will we see the jewels?" he asked.

"What jewels?" said the Captain.

He speared a clam with his fork.

"Why, the jewels on the mainland," said the Komodo Dragon. "The ones that twinkle at night."

"*Twinkle*?" said the Captain. "At night?"

He turned to stare at Miss Mildew.

"GOOD HEAVENS!" he yelled. "YOU'RE NOT MISS MILDEW!"

"Who's Miss Mildew?" asked the Komodo Dragon.

The Captain leaped in the air. The table fell over with a crash. The tourists jumped up on their chairs. Everybody was shouting.

gulp (GULP) a big swallow

"Dinner must be over," said the Komodo Dragon. "I think I'll take a stroll on deck and enjoy the evening air."

He went outside and looked at the moon. "It's so peaceful here," he said.

The tourists and the Captain ran below. They hid in the engine room.

"Where *is* everybody?" said the Komodo Dragon, looking about.

He strolled over to the Captain's bridge.

"Why, no one's steering the ship!" he said. "We might crash into some rocks. Captain! Oh, Captain!" he called.

The Captain was hiding behind the pump, and the tourists lay under the pipes.

"They must have all gone to bed," said the Komodo Dragon. "I'll steer the ship into harbor myself."

He rang the ship's bell. Dong! Dong! Dong! And blew the ship's whistle. Wheeeeeeeoooo! And then he sailed the ship into the bay.

The lights along the shore twinkled brightly.

"How wonderful!" cried the Komodo Dragon, looking out the window. "The jewels are very large! And how brightly they shine!"

Honk! Honk! Honk! The harbor police boat pulled alongside.

---

stroll (STROHL) a walk

bridge (BRIJ) the place on a ship from which it is controlled

steering (STEER-ing) driving or guiding

"Where do you think you're going?" shouted the Police Captain, stamping up the deck. His police badge shone in the moonlight, and he waved his flashlight in the air.

"I beg your pardon," said the Komodo Dragon. "Am I sailing too close to the shore?"

"Great Scott!" cried the Police Captain. "There's a lizard steering that ship! He must have eaten the Captain and everyone on board! Open fire!"

Bang! Bang! Bang!

"Do I hear firecrackers?" said the Komodo Dragon. "It must be a <u>celebration</u>!"

He waved to the police boat. "I wish I could stay,"

<u>celebration</u> (sel-u-BRAY-shun) a party

12

he called, "but I've seen the jewels and now it's time for me to go home again. Good-bye!"

He turned the ship around and sailed, full speed ahead, out of the harbor.

Dong! Dong! Dong! Wheeeeeeeooooooo! His ship sailed slowly over the sea under the shining stars.

"The moon is yellow tonight," said the Komodo Dragon, "and it's left a ribbon of light on the waves to guide us safely home."

At last he dropped anchor in his bay.

"Home again," he yawned. "What a wonderful trip it's been!"

He let down a rowboat over the side and rowed himself to shore.

Miss Mildew was wading about near the beach.

"Where have you been?" she shouted. "I've been waiting here for hours!"

Trumpet flowers hung from her hat.

"We've been to see the jewels," said the Komodo Dragon, climbing out of the boat. "They're very large and shiny!"

Miss Mildew's hat hung over her eyes.

"Give me the oars!" she yelled. And she rowed herself out to the ship and climbed aboard.

The Komodo Dragon watched the ship sail slowly out of the bay. Then he climbed up to his favorite rock and waited for the dawn.

The faraway lights twinkled faintly in the distance. The Komodo Dragon smiled.

"There they are," he yawned sleepily. "And to think I've been there myself!"

He curled his great green tail about him, and he dreamed of jewels all morning long.

■ Talk About the Story

1. How was the Komodo Dragon able to get control of the ship?

2. How might the story be different if the crew and passengers had stayed calm?

3. Why did it take so long for people to notice there was a lizard aboard the ship?

4. What do you think was the most surprising part of the story? Tell why you think so.

5. Could a story like "The Komodo Dragon's Jewels" take place in your home town? Why or why not?

■ Think About the Story

1. How might the story be different if the Komodo Dragon had thought the lights from the mainland were stars instead of jewels?

2. Suppose Miss Mildew was telling the story. How would it be different?

3. How would the story end if the police captured the Komodo Dragon?

4. In what ways were Miss Mildew and the Komodo Dragon alike?

■ Write About the Story

Imagine that you were the waiter who saw the Komodo Dragon. Write a paragraph telling what you would do and why.

Understanding Plot

■ Reading About Plot

Many things happen in "The Komodo Dragon's Jewels." Together, these happenings, or events, make up the plot of the story.

Different stories have different plots, but most plots are alike in one important way. They have a beginning, a turning point, and an end. The turning point is often the most exciting part of the story. It is a clue to how the story will end. The events at the beginning of a story build to the turning point. The events after the turning point explain how the story ends.

■ Thinking About Plot

Below is a list of events in "The Komodo Dragon's Jewels." Decide which event is the turning point of the story and why.

1. A tourist ship visits the Komodo Dragon's island.
2. The Komodo Dragon rows to the ship.
3. The captain discovers the Komodo Dragon.
4. Everyone on the ship hides from the dragon.
5. The dragon steers the ship toward the jewels.
6. The dragon sees the jewels and heads for home.

The turning point of the story is when the captain discovers the Komodo Dragon. The events that come before build up to this. Once the dragon is discovered, everyone hides. Then, the dragon is able to get what it wants—a look at the jewels. After that the story ends quickly.

■ Using What You Have Learned

Read the cartoon. Then answer the questions.

What is the plot of the story?
What is the turning point?
What helped you decide on the turning point?

As you read, be on the look-out for the turning point in the plot of a story. You will be helping yourself to better understand and enjoy what you are reading.

The Komodo Dragon gave the tourists the biggest surprise of their lives. In "Who's a Pest?" Little Homer does the surprising. In the end, his actions surprise everyone, including himself.

WHO'S A PEST?

by CROSBY NEWELL BONSALL

Lolly, Molly, Polly, and Dolly all looked at Homer. Homer was their brother.

"I didn't do it," said Homer.

"Yes, you did," they said. "Yes, you did. And you're a pest!"

Then Lolly and Molly and Polly and Dolly all turned their backs.

"Beans," said Homer, "I'm not a pest." But Lolly, Molly, Polly, and Dolly walked away.

Down by the woodpile Homer said again, "I'm not a pest!"

"I never said you were," said a lizard.

"I never said you said I was," said Homer.

"I never said you said I said you were," said the lizard.

"I never said you said I said you said I was," said Homer.

"Said what?" asked the lizard.

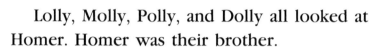

pest (PEST) a person who bothers others

18

"Said I was a pest," said Homer.

"Who?" asked the lizard.

"You," said Homer.

"Me?" said the lizard, "I'm no pest."

"I never said you were," said Homer.

"I never said you said I was," said the lizard.

"Beans," said Homer.

"You started it," said the lizard.

"You are a pest!"

And the lizard slipped away.

"Beans," said Homer, "I'm not a pest."

He ran all the way down a hill and met a chipmunk.

"What time is it?" asked the chipmunk.

"Ten to two," said Homer.

"Ten to who?" asked the chipmunk.

"Not who—what," said Homer.

"Ten to what?" asked the chipmunk.

"Yes," said Homer.

"YES," cried the chipmunk, "what kind of time is that?"

"It isn't the time," Homer said.

"But I asked for the time," said the chipmunk.

"I told you," said Homer.

"What?" asked the chipmunk.

"The time," said Homer.

"What time?" asked the chipmunk.

"The time it was then," said Homer.

"When was then?" asked the chipmunk.

"Then was when you asked me," said Homer.

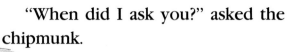

"When did I ask you?" asked the chipmunk.

"At ten to two," said Homer.

"But that was then," said the chipmunk.

"What time is it now?"

"Two to two," said Homer.

"Don't toot at me," said the chipmunk.

"You're a pest!"

And the chipmunk ran away.

"Beans," said Homer, "I'm not a pest!"

"No one ever thinks he's a pest," said a rabbit.

"You can't tell about yourself."

"I can tell about myself," said Homer.

"*They* can't tell about myself."

"About me," said the rabbit.

"You?" asked Homer.

"They can't tell about *me,*" said the rabbit.

"You, too?" asked Homer.

"No, you," said the rabbit.

"They can't tell about you."

"That's what I said," said Homer.

"Now what shall I do?"

"I'm glad you asked me," said the rabbit.
"I'm not a pest, so I shall be able to tell you
how *not* to be a pest."

"Okay," said Homer.

"Stay out of gardens," said the rabbit.

"But I don't go into gardens," Homer said.

"Well, stay out of them, anyway," said the
rabbit.

"But if I'm not in, how can I stay out?"
Homer asked.

"It's easy," said the rabbit.

"You can stay out by not going in."

"But I *am* out," Homer said.

"You're lucky," said the rabbit, "you got out in time."

"But I was never in," said Homer.

"Oh, hush," said the rabbit, "The others were right. You *are* a pest!" And the rabbit hopped away.

"Beans," said Homer, "I'm not a pest!"

Homer sat down. Soon he heard a sound.

"Help," it said. "Help! Help! Help!"

Homer looked around.

"Help who?" he asked.

"Help me," said the sound.

"Who's me?" Homer asked.

"Me is me. I don't know who *you* are," said the sound.

"I'm Homer," said Homer.

"Please help me, Homer," said the sound.

"Where are you?" cried Homer.

"Here," said the sound.

"Where's here?" asked Homer.

"Here is here," said the sound.

"Oh, my," cried Homer, "I'll never find you. I don't know where here is."

"Then find someone who does," cried the sound.

Just then the rabbit came along.

"You must help me," Homer cried.

"Oh, it's you," said the rabbit. "What a pest!"

"Me is lost," Homer cried.

"You don't look lost to me," said the rabbit.

"I'm not lost," Homer said, "Me is."

"Who is Me?" asked the rabbit.

"You are the rabbit." Homer said.

"I know that," snapped the rabbit. "Who is the Me you're talking about?"

"He says he is Me," Homer said.

"Well, if he says he is you," said the rabbit, "we must find you. And here you are!"

The chipmunk ran by and stopped.

"Please help us," Homer said.

"Oh, it's you," said the chipmunk. "What a pest!"

"He wants us to find Me," said the rabbit.

"Find you?" said the chipmunk. "You are here!"

"No, no," cried the rabbit. "Me is here."

"That's what I said," cried the chipmunk.

"What did you say?" asked the lizard. He slipped from behind a tree.

"He said he was here," Homer said.

"Oh, it's you," said the lizard. "What a pest! Who's here?" he asked.

"Me," said the rabbit.

"HELP!" said the sound.

"What is that?" cried the rabbit and the chipmunk and the lizard.

"That is Me," said Homer.

"You!" they cried.

"No, ME," cried the sound. "I'm here."

---

snapped (SNAPT) spoke sharply

Lolly and Molly and Polly and Dolly
skipped by. They saw Homer. "Oh, it's you,"
they said. "What a pest!"

But Homer didn't hear. He and the rabbit
and the chipmunk and the lizard were
looking all over.

"What are you looking for?" asked Lolly,
Molly, Polly, and Dolly.

"Not what, who," Homer said.

"Not who, whom," said the rabbit.

"Whom what?" asked the girls.

"Whom are you looking for?" said the
chipmunk.

"We're not looking for anyone," said Lolly,
Molly, Polly, and Dolly.

"Well, start looking for ME,"
said the sound.

Lolly took a step back.

Crash!

Lolly wasn't there anymore.
Molly went to look.

Crash!

Molly wasn't there anymore. Polly ran over.

Crash!

Polly wasn't there anymore. Dolly ran after
Polly.

Crash!

Dolly wasn't there anymore.

"This is silly," said the rabbit. He hopped
over.

Crash!

The rabbit wasn't there anymore. The
chipmunk went after him.

Crash!

The chipmunk wasn't there anymore.

"Well," said the lizard, "it's my turn now."

Crash!

The lizard wasn't there anymore.

"HELP!" cried the sound. "Help! Help! Help! Help!" cried Lolly, Molly, Polly, and Dolly.

"Help!" cried the rabbit and the chipmunk and the lizard.

"I think I'll go home," said Homer.

But if he went home without his sisters, his mother would say, "Well, Homer, where are your sisters? Where are Lolly and Molly and Polly and Dolly?"

And Homer would say, "In a hole."

And think of the lizard. And all the little lizards waiting for their father. And their father was in a hole.

And think of the chipmunk. And all the little chipmunks waiting for their father. And their father was in a hole.

And think of the rabbit. And all the little rabbits waiting for their father. And their father was in a hole.

And think of the sound, whatever it was. And all the little whatevers waiting for their father. And their father was in a hole.

So Homer got them all out. How? Easy as pie. This is what he told them:

"Lizard, sit on the chipmunk. Chipmunk, sit on the rabbit. Rabbit, sit on Lolly, Lolly, sit on Molly, Molly, sit on Polly. Polly, sit on Dolly. Dolly, sit on whatever is making the sound."

And then—

Homer pulled the lizard who pulled the chipmunk who pulled the rabbit who pulled Lolly and Molly and Polly and Dolly who pulled and pulled whatever it was.

What was it?

It was a bear.

"I'm a pest," he said.

"No! No! No! No!" said Lolly and Molly and Polly and Dolly.

"No!" said the lizard and the chipmunk.

"No, indeed," said the rabbit, "there's the pest," and he looked at Homer.

"Not at all," said the bear. "He got me out."

"He did not, I did," snapped the rabbit.

"You did not, I did," cried the chipmunk.

"You are both wrong, I did," said the lizard.

"No, we did," cried Lolly and Molly and Polly and Dolly.

"I don't see how," said the bear. "You were all in the hole with me."

"Oh," said the rabbit.

"Mmmm," said the chipmunk.

"Uh," said the lizard.

Lolly looked at the sky. Molly looked at her toes. Polly looked at her nails. And Dolly rubbed her nose.

"Now," said the bear, "I fell in a hole. I made a lot of fuss so—that makes me a pest.

You each fell in the hole. You each made a
lot of fuss. So—that makes each of you a
pest!"

The bear looked at Homer. "There is just
one who is not a pest."

"Who is that?" asked Homer.

"Well, if you don't know," snapped the
rabbit.

"We won't tell you," cried the chipmunk.

"Right," said the lizard. "What a pest!"

"Beans," said Homer. "I'm not a pest!"

"Right! Right! Right! Right!" said Lolly,
Molly, Polly, and Dolly.

"That's what *I* said," said the lizard.

"Said what?" asked the rabbit.

"Said who?" asked the chipmunk.

"I didn't say anything," said the bear.

"We didn't say you did," said Lolly and
Molly and Polly and Dolly.

"I didn't say you said I did," said the lizard.

"Yes, you did," said the rabbit.

"You keep out of this," snapped the
chipmunk. "You're a pest!"

Homer and bear walked away.

"You see how it is," said the bear.

"I see how it is," said Homer.

He looked back.

"Hey," he yelled, "YOU'RE ALL PESTS!"

Then Homer and the bear ran off over
the hill.

■ Talk About the Story

1. What was Homer's problem?

2. What happened that gave Homer a chance to solve his problem?

3. What did Homer do that surprised everyone, including himself?

4. Did Homer's actions help solve his problem? How do you know?

5. Who are the pests in the story? What does each pest say that makes you think so?

■ Think About the Story

1. Think of some different ways that Homer could have helped the others out of the hole.

2. Have you ever known someone who you thought was a pest? Describe them.

3. Has anyone ever called you a pest? How did it make you feel?

4. How do you think the hole that everyone fell into got there in the first place?

■ Write About the Story

Write a new ending to the story. Imagine that Homer went home without his sisters. Tell what happened.

Spotlight on

Crosby
Newell Bonsall

Crosby Newell Bonsall didn't plan to write and illustrate children's books. It happened by accident.

After college, she worked for different advertising companies. One day, she was at her drawing board. As she stopped to think about something, she doodled. A doll manufacturer saw the doodle and liked it. Soon, there was a whole family of doodle dolls. These were the characters for Crosby Newell Bonsall's first book. She has been writing and illustrating stories ever since.

Look back at the illustrations for "Who's a Pest." Like many of Bonsall's pictures, they tell a story all their own.

Other Books Written and Illustrated by
Crosby Newell Bonsall

It's Mine!   *The Surprise Party*
I Mean It Stanley   *Hurry Up, Slowpoke*
                               The Case of the Hungry Stranger

The Centipede

by JACK PRELUTSKY

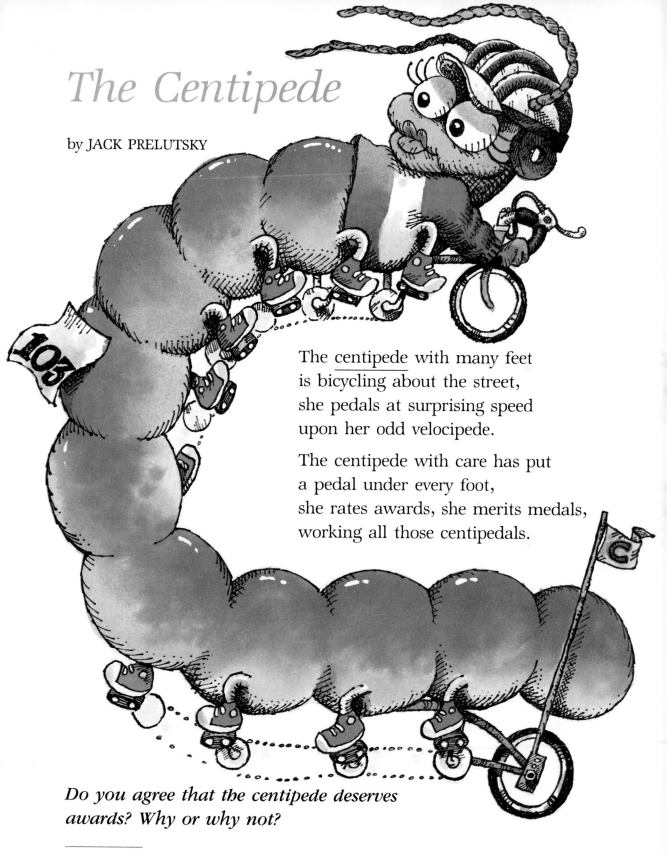

The centipede with many feet
is bicycling about the street,
she pedals at surprising speed
upon her odd velocipede.

The centipede with care has put
a pedal under every foot,
she rates awards, she merits medals,
working all those centipedals.

*Do you agree that the centipede deserves
awards? Why or why not?*

centipede (SEN-tih-peed) an insect that looks like a worm with many legs

Sea Song

by MARCHETTE CHUTE

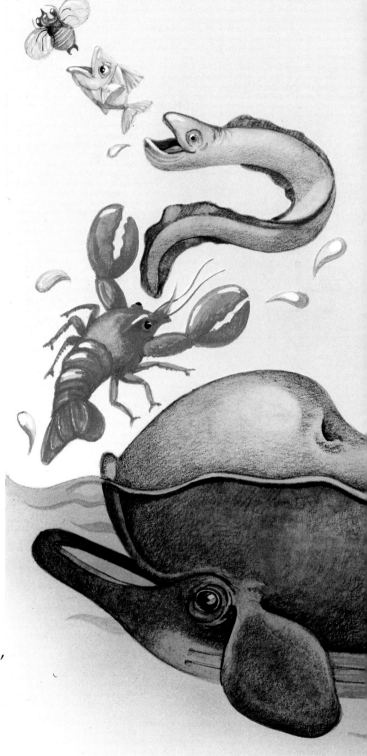

Once a little doodle bug
  Ran away,
Jumped in the ocean
  For the day.

Along came a <u>minnow</u>,
  Small and brown;
Saw the little doodle bug,
  Gulped him down.

Here is the minnow,
  Grown rather fat:

Here is the <u>eel</u> who
  Ate her for that:

Along came a lobster,
  Saw that happy eel;
Looked at her thoughtfully,
  Changed her to a meal.

<u>minnow</u> (MIN-oh) a very small fish

<u>eel</u> (EEL) a slippery fish that looks like a snake

Here is the lobster,
  Trying to hide:
Here is a whale with
  The lobster inside:

A little boy out fishing
  Saw a tail;
Pulled at the other end,
  Up came the whale.

THEN
Out came the doddle bug,
  Flapping his wings;
Out came the lobster
  And all the other things.

They looked at each other
  With nothing to say.
They turned from each other
  And jumped in the bay.
All except the doodle bug;
  He flew away.

Tell the story of the sea
song in your own words.

Homer surprised everyone with his idea that saved the day. In "Mitzi Takes a Taxi," Mitzi has a make-believe adventure that leaves her surprised and tired before the day even begins.

Mitzi Takes a Taxi

by LORE SEGAL

"Tell me a story," said Martha.

Once upon a time (said her mother) there was a Mitzi. She had a mother and a father and a brother who was a baby. His name was Jacob.

One morning Mitzi woke up. Jacob was in his <u>crib</u>, asleep. Mitzi went and looked in her mother and father's room. They were asleep.

She looked in the living room. There was nobody there. There was nobody in the kitchen.

Mitzi went back into the children's room, shook the crib and said, "Jacob, are you asleep?"

Jacob said, "Dadadadadadada."

"Good," said Mitzi. "What shall we do?"

"Let's go to Grandma and Grandpa's house," said Jacob.

"Right," said Mitzi. "Let's go."

"First make me my bottle," said Jacob. So Mitzi got Jacob's bottle, carried it into the kitchen and opened

—————————
<u>crib</u> (KRIB) a young child's bed

32

the refrigerator and took out a carton of milk and opened it and took the top off Jacob's bottle and poured in the milk and put the top back on and closed the carton and put it back in the refrigerator and closed the door and carried the bottle into the children's room and gave it to Jacob and said, "Let's go."

Jacob said, "Change my diaper." So Mitzi climbed into Jacob's crib and took his pajamas off and took off his rubber pants and took the pins out of his diaper and climbed out of the crib and put the diaper in the diaper pail and took a fresh diaper and climbed into the crib and put the diaper on Jacob and put in the pins and put on a fresh pair of rubber pants and Jacob said,

"Dress me." So Mitzi lifted Jacob out of the crib and put him on the floor and she put on his shirt and his overalls and his socks. She put on his right shoe and his left shoe and his snowsuit and his mittens and tied his hat under his chin and said, "*Now,* let's go."

Jacob said, "In your pajamas?"

When Mitzi had got on her shirt and her skirt and her socks and her shoes and put herself into her snowsuit and found her mittens and tied her hat under her chin, Jacob said, "Now, let's go."

Mitzi put Jacob in his stroller and pushed the stroller out of their front door and down the hall to the elevator.

pajamas (puh-JA-muz) clothes to sleep in

overalls (OH-ver-awlz) pants with a bib and straps

stroller (STROH-ler) a seat with wheels in which a baby sits

"Only I can reach the button," she said.

"Take me out and hold me up," said Jacob. So Mitzi took Jacob out of the stroller and held him way up and Jacob pressed the button. When the elevator came, Mitzi pushed the stroller in, the door closed and the elevator went down to the ground floor and the door opened.

The doorman in the lobby said, "Good morning, Mitzi. Good morning, Jacob."

Jacob said, "Dadadada."

Mitzi said, "We're going to Grandma and Grandpa's house."

The doorman helped Mitzi take the stroller down the steps and Mitzi pushed Jacob to the corner of the street and called, "TAXI!"

A taxi stopped and the driver got out and came around to their side. He lifted Jacob out of the stroller and put him in the back seat and lifted Mitzi in and folded up the stroller and put it in the empty front seat and walked around to his side and got in and said, "Where to?"

"Grandma and Grandpa's house, please," said Mitzi.

"Where do they live?" asked the driver.

"I don't know," said Mitzi.

So the driver got out and came around to the other side and took the stroller from the front seat and unfolded it on the sidewalk and took Jacob out and put him in the stroller and took Mitzi out and put her on the sidewalk and walked around to his side and got in and drove away.

Mitzi pushed Jacob back to the house.

The doorman helped her get the stroller up the stairs and he pushed the elevator button for them. They got out on their floor and went in their front door and into their room. Mitzi took Jacob out of the stroller and untied his hat and took off his mittens. She took off his snowsuit and his right shoe and his left shoe and his socks and his overalls and his shirt and put on his pajamas and lifted him into his crib. Then she undressed herself and put her pajamas on and got back into bed and covered herself up and then the alarm clock rang in her mother and father's room.

Mitzi's mother came into the children's room and said, "Good morning, Mitzi," and Mitzi said, "Morning, Mommy," and her mother said, "Good morning, Jacob," and Jacob said, "Dadadada."

"Come to Mommy, Jacob," said his mother. "I'll get you a nice bottle and change your diaper," and she took him out of the crib and she said, "Mitzi, today can you be a *really big* girl and take off your *own* pajamas all by yourself?"

"You do it," said Mitzi, "I'm exhausted."

"Exhausted, are you!" said her mother. "How come you're exhausted so early in the morning?"

"Because I am," said Mitzi. "Mommy! Where do Grandma and Grandpa live?"

"Six West Seventy-Seventh Street," said her mother. "Why do you ask?"

"Because," said Mitzi.

exhausted (ig-ZAWST-ed) very tired

■ Talk About the Story

1. Which parts of the story were real? Which parts were make-believe? What clues in the story helped you decide?

2. Why would the taxi driver need to know Grandpa's address?

3. What are some of the things that surprised Mitzi? What surprised Mitzi's mother?

4. What are some things you know about Mitzi from reading the story?

5. How might the story be different if it took place in a small town?

■ Think About the Story

1. Why do you think Jacob wanted to go to Grandma and Grandpa's house?

2. Suppose Mitzi and Jacob had gotten lost? How could they find their way home?

3. In what way would the story be different if Jacob was older than Mitzi?

4. Who is it that is telling the story about Mitzi?

■ Write About the Story

Write directions for a taxi driver. Tell the driver where you want to go and how to get there.

Until now, the story characters have had all the surprises. Now, it's your turn. Get ready for a surprise in "The Browns Take the Day Off."

The Browns Take the Day Off

retold by ALVIN SCHWARTZ

It was a hot day. So Mr. Brown took his family to the swimming pool. Sam and Jane jumped right in. They raced all the way to the other end of the pool. Then they raced back.

Grandpa jumped in. Then he jumped up and down. Each time he came down he called out, "Brrrrrrrrr!"

Mr. Brown bounced up and down on the diving board. Mrs. Brown sat in the sun and turned bright red.

"It is very nice here today," said Jane.

"It will be even nicer on Tuesday," said the man with the broom.

"Why?" asked Sam.

"Why?" asked Grandpa.

"Why?" asked Mr. Brown.

"On Tuesday," said the man with the broom, "there will be water in the pool."

■ Talk About the Story

1. What is the surprise at the end of the story?
2. How does the illustrator help keep the ending a surprise?

■ Think About the Story

1. How would you have fun at a pool with no water?
2. What do you think the man with the broom thought of the Brown family?
3. What silly things do you think the Browns might do on a cold winter day?

■ Write About the Story

Make up a joke with a 'punch line' or think of one you have heard. Write the joke as part of a letter to a friend.

Enjoying Fiction

Fiction is stories about characters and events that are not real. Some fiction is fantasy—stories about things that couldn't possibly happen. Other fiction is realistic. It is stories about people and things that could be real.

Think about the fiction in this unit. Which stories are fantasy? Which are realistic? What helped you decide?

Look at the story characters below. Which seem real? Which are fantasy? Write a story about one of the characters.

As you read the next story, decide if it is fantasy or realistic fiction.

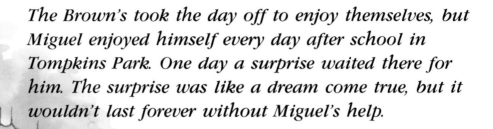

The Brown's took the day off to enjoy themselves, but Miguel enjoyed himself every day after school in Tompkins Park. One day a surprise waited there for him. The surprise was like a dream come true, but it wouldn't last forever without Miguel's help.

Miguel's Mountain

by BILL BINZEN

A mountain road twists and turns, and climbs up and down and around.

But a city street goes straight ahead, as far as the eye can see.

Miguel lives on a city street. He knows that street well, for he has never been out of the city.

One day, Miguel's teacher read an old fairy tale about a king who lived in a great castle high on a mountaintop.

Miguel was so interested in the story that he didn't even know when the class was over. "I would love to climb a mountain!" he thought to himself.

Every day after school, Miguel raced to the park down the block.

The park was great fun! Miguel knew lots of the boys and girls who played there.

One day some workmen came to the park. They brought a steamshovel with them. The steamshovel worked very hard scooping up dirt to make a hole for a new building in the park. The hole got deeper and the dirt piled higher. Finally, the workmen and their steamshovel went away.

That afternoon, Miguel went to the park as usual. Some of his friends were on the huge pile of dirt. Suddenly Miguel had an idea.

He raced up, up, up to the top of the pile.

"It's a mountain!" he shouted. "It's a mountain, and I'm the king of the mountain!"

In no time at all, that mountain was covered with boys. Up the mountain they ran, down and around and around and up, all afternoon.

Every day after that, more children were on the mountain than any place else in the park.

Sometimes they would charge off it on wild horses . . . and often a frontier war would break out between the Indians and Cowboys.

There were blinding dust storms . . . and games of Ring-Around-the-Rosy.

It was fun taking the roller coaster down . . . and then playing Follow-the-Leader coming back up.

Then one day, an alarming story spread through the park. Gregory heard it first. He told Abby, and she told Eric. Eric told Susanna, and Susanna told Miguel.

Miguel couldn't believe it. For a moment he stood very still. Then he ran home as fast as he could, for he had to do something to keep back the tears.

For hours he sat by the window, lost in thought. It was dark when his mother came home.

"What's the matter, Miguel?" she asked. "I've never seen you look so sad."

"In three days they're going to take away the mountain," Miguel answered. "They're going to take it away forever!"

Miguel's mother patted him on the head. "I know how you feel about that mountain," she said kindly, "but there's nothing we can do. I don't believe anyone could save it."

frontier (frun-TEER) a border
blinding (BLYND-ing) making it impossible to see
alarming (uh-LARM-ing) frightening

And then she went to the kitchen to start supper.

Miguel thought about the mountain long into the night. Suddenly, he sat straight up in bed. "I've got an idea," he said to himself. "At least it's worth a try."

And he fell asleep at last.

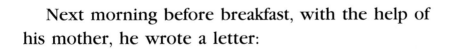

Next morning before breakfast, with the help of his mother, he wrote a letter:

> Dear Mr. Mayor,
>   Please don't let them take away the mountain in Tompkins Park. We children play on it every single day.
>   Love,
>   Miguel

He carefully addressed the envelope. On the front in large letters he wrote "TO THE MAYOR," and on the back he put his own name and address.

Miguel knocked on the door of his friend, Robert, on his way downstairs. He told Robert all about the letter he had just written.

The two boys raced off to the post office, as fast as their legs would carry them.

Carefully they mailed the letter in the right slot and hurried off to school.

The next two days were very difficult for Miguel. It was hard to pay attention to his schoolwork. When the teacher asked him, "What is four and three?" he said, "Eight." The third day was the worst. On the third day the mountain would disappear forever.

That afternoon, Miguel's teacher said, "Let's paint some pictures."

Usually, Miguel loved to paint. He loved to use the bright colors. But this time it was different. Miguel just sat and looked at his paper and didn't paint a thing.

After school Miguel walked slowly home. He took the long way because he couldn't bear to look into the park. He decided that he didn't want to go there ever again.

For a long time, Miguel sat on the front steps of the house next door. He didn't feel like doing anything else.

"Bet you can't jump over the fire hydrant!" shouted Peter as he came running out of the house.

But Miguel wouldn't even try. He just stared at the ground.

---

disappear (dis-uh-PEER) to go out of sight

Sometime later two extra large feet appeared right under his nose. Miguel looked up.

A tall man with a friendly face was gazing down at him. "Do you know Miguel Garcia?" he asked.

"I'm Miguel Garcia," Miguel said.

"Then you must be the boy who wrote the Mayor a letter about the mountain," said the man.

"Yes, I am," Miguel said, feeling excited, though he wasn't sure why.

"Well," said the man, smiling, "I have good news for you, Miguel! You see, after the Mayor read your letter, he had a talk with the man in charge of parks. They both agreed that your idea was a very good one.

"So they have asked me to tell you that your mountain will stay right where it is forever!"

gazing (GAYZ-ing) staring

At first Miguel couldn't say anything. But he knew how to smile, and right then and there his face lit up with the biggest grin the man had ever seen.

Finally, Miguel got his tongue back. "Thank you, mister," he said. "That's great news!"

Miguel raced off to the park. He forgot that only a few short hours before he had decided never to go there again.

"Great news! Great news!" Miguel shouted. Soon all the boys and girls had crowded around him. Miguel told them everything the man had said.

As he finished, they all started talking at once.

"Let's have a parade to celebrate!" yelled Peter.

"Yes, and with music too," said Jenny.

"Good idea!" everyone shouted.

And so it was arranged.

Tom brought a drum, and Ira brought a horn. Carmen had a tambourine and Eric brought his big brother's trumpet.

tambourine (tam-bor-EEN) a kind of musical instrument

What a time they had then! They paraded all through the park, down every last path.

Eric was in the lead. He marched them up to the top of the hill and marched them down again.

Up and down they went, again and again, to the tooting of trumpets and the banging of drums.

Finally, they marched to the top of the mountain and came to a halt.

For a moment, at the top, there was a lot of whispering. Then, in voices so loud that they could be heard all over the park, everyone sang,

"Hooray for Miguel!
Hooray for Miguel!
He saved the mountain!
Isn't that swell!"

It was getting dark, and slowly the boys and girls went home one by one.

---
halt (HAWLT) to stop

Early next morning, two small figures could be
seen racing to the top of the mountain. At the
summit, they placed a flag.

"This really makes it official,' said Eric. "From now
on this will always be known as "Miguel's Mountain."

Miguel didn't say anything. He just smiled.

---

summit (SUM-it) the top

■ Talk About the Story

1. What did Miguel and his friends have fun doing every day after school?

2. What was the problem that was going to spoil their fun?

3. How was the problem solved?

4. Do you think Miguel deserved to have the mountain named after him? Why or why not?

5. Could "Miguel's Mountain" have taken place somewhere besides a big city? Why or why not?

6. What story event probably surprised Miguel the most?

■ Think About the Story

1. Do you think it took courage for Miguel to write a letter to the mayor? Why or why not?

2. What would have happened if the mayor did not think Miguel's idea was a good one?

3. How do you behave when you are worried or sad?

4. How would you feel if someone named a mountain after you?

■ Write About the Story

Imagine that your favorite playground is going to be turned into a parking lot. Help save the playground by writing a letter to the mayor.

"At the Library"

To learn more about the story characters in this unit, find the books listed below in your school library. You may be surprised at the fun you'll have.

1. ***The Komodo Dragon's Jewels,*** by Diane Redfield Massey. Published by MacMillan Publishing Company in 1975.

2. ***Miguel's Mountain,*** by Bill Binzen. Published by Coward-McCann in 1968.

3. ***Tell Me A Mitzi,*** by Lore Segal. Published by Farrar, Straus & Giroux in 1970.

4. ***There's a Carrot in My Ear,*** by Alvin Schwartz. Published by Harper & Row in 1982.

5. ***Who's A Pest?,*** by Crosby Newall Bonsall. Published by Harper & Row in 1962.

Troubles

Where there is smoke, there is fire. Where there is fire, there is trouble. But almost anything can mean trouble—even an overcoat or a piece of cheese.

The story characters in this unit get themselves into all kinds of trouble. Perhaps you can help them find a way out.

Which do you think is stronger, the sun or the wind? These two characters cause some trouble when they try to find out.

THE SUN AND THE WIND

by SALLY JARVIS

Players

WIND
SUN
MAN

WIND: Oh, how strong I am! I am stronger than the sun!

SUN: Oh, no, Mr. Wind. I am stronger than you.

WIND: Let us see. Look at that man, He is in a black coat.

SUN: I see him.

WIND: Let us see who can make that man take off his coat.

SUN: All right. You may go first.

WIND: Whooooooooooooooooo!

MAN: Oh, how cold it is! *(He holds on to his coat.)*

WIND: Whooooooooooo! I want that coat!

MAN: Oh, me! What a strong wind! *(He buttons his coat.)*

WIND: Whooooooo! I WANT THAT COAT!

MAN: I am so cold! I will get *two* coats!

WIND: Well, Sun, if I cannot blow his coat off you cannot shine it off.

SUN: We will see. *(He shines on the man.)*

MAN: Now I am not so cold. *(Sun shines on the man.)*

MAN: What a funny day. First it is cold. Now it is hot. *(He unbuttons his coat. Sun shines and shines.)*

MAN: Now I am too hot. I will take off my coat.

WIND: Well, Mr. Sun. The man took off his coat for you. Maybe there is more than one way to be strong!

■ Talk About the Story

1. Who are the characters in this play?
2. What did the sun and the wind do to find out which of them was stronger?
3. Who won the contest? Why?
4. What did the wind learn from the contest?

■ Think About the Story

1. How do you think the man in this play felt?
2. Who do you think would win in a contest to make the man put on his coat, the sun or the wind?
3. Describe the weather on the day this play takes place.

■ Write About the Story

Both the wind and the sun bragged about how strong they were. Now it's your turn to boast! Decide on something to brag about. Then put your boast in writing.

Enjoying Plays

Plays are stories written using only dialogue. They are meant to be read aloud or acted out on a stage. In a play, the audience learns about the story events by listening to what the characters say and by watching what they do.

Reading a play is different from watching a play. Look back at "The Sun and the Wind." How did you know what each character said? What helped you find out what each character did?

Study the cartoon below. Write the cartoon as if it were a play.

As you read the next play, use your imagination. Try to 'see' it and 'hear' it while you read it.

*The boastful wind created troubles when he and the
sun tried to solve a problem. In "Which Piece is Mine?"
the rabbit and the cat get into trouble when they ask
someone else to solve a problem.*

Which Piece is Mine?

by BARBARA WALKER

Players

CAT
RABBIT
FOX

*(The cat and the rabbit are good friends. One day
in the forest they find a big piece of cheese.
They both like cheese very much.)*

CAT: You break the cheese into two pieces. Then we
will each have a piece.

RABBIT: I will make the pieces exactly the same size.
*(He breaks the cheese into two pieces. But one
piece is a little bigger than the other.)*

CAT: *(grabbing the bigger piece)* This piece is mine.

RABBIT: No it isn't. It's mine! *(A fox walks by.)*

RABBIT: Mr. Fox, we have two pieces of cheese. I
want the bigger piece. The cat wants the bigger
piece. Which piece is mine?

58

FOX: That's easy. I'll bite the bigger piece so they will both be the same. *(He bites the cheese, but he bites off too much.)*

CAT: Now the other piece is bigger!

FOX: That's all right. I will bite that one so they will both be the same size. *(But he bites off too much again.)*

RABBIT: Now the first one is bigger again.

FOX: I will bite it again. Then they will be the same size. *(This time he eats the whole piece.)*

CAT: But it's all gone now!

FOX: So it is. Now I will have to eat the other one. Then they will surely be the same size. *(He eats the other piece, and he runs away, happy and full of cheese.)*

RABBIT: Now both pieces are gone!

CAT: Yes, and which piece was mine?

RABBIT: It doesn't matter now. They are both gone, and we don't have any cheese at all.

CAT: From now on let us solve our problems ourselves!

■ Talk About the Story

1. What problem did the cat and the rabbit have?
2. How did they decide to solve that problem?
3. What happened to the cheese? Why?
4. Do you think the fox really wanted to help the cat and the rabbit? Why or why not?

■ Think About the Story

1. Where do you think this play takes place? In a restaurant, in a field, under water? Why?
2. We usually think of a fox as being sly. What if other kinds of animals had come along? How would a wise owl have solved the problem? Or a stubborn mule? Or a grouchy bear?
3. How would this play be different if it were written as a story?

■ Write About the Story

Imagine that you write an advice column for a newspaper. The cat and the rabbit have written a letter to you. They have asked you for advice on how best to share a piece of cheese equally. Write an answer to the cat and the rabbit in your advice column. Give them some ideas on how to solve their problem.

The cat and the rabbit have some troubles over a piece of cheese. But Ilse, in "The Sod House," finds herself with troubles that may mean life or death.

THE SOD HOUSE

by ELIZABETH COATSWORTH

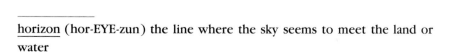

One hot afternoon when the wind was blowing from the south, Ilse was puzzled to see that a black cloud was coming up over the curving <u>horizon</u> of the prairie.

"There's going to be rain," she called to Papa and Mama, who were inside the house. Papa came to the door to look.

The cloud was very black and it was moving fast. Already it was towering above the prairie, and the sunlit grass and flowers seemed very bright against it.

A rabbit came bounding past the house, never glancing at them. Another followed. Then a flock of birds flew by, <u>uttering</u> cries of alarm.

<u>horizon</u> (hor-EYE-zun) the line where the sky seems to meet the land or water

<u>uttering</u> (UT-ur-ing) speaking

The black cloud was whirling upwards as it approached. Mama came to the door.

"I smell smoke, Friedrich!" she cried.

"You are right, Maria! The prairie's on fire!" Papa said. "Close the doors and windows while I get Little Peter! We'll be safe by the river."

That day Little Peter was picketed to one side of the house by himself. Papa ran and brought him back, snorting and fidgeting. It was hard to keep him still long enough to get Mama on his back. When Papa lifted Hans into her arms, Little Peter jumped and Hans hit his head against her shoulder and began to cry. Papa swung Ilse up behind Mama.

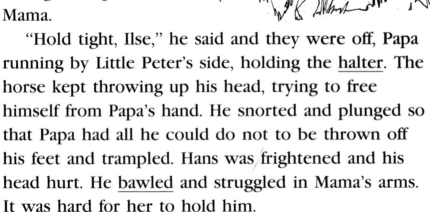

"Hold tight, Ilse," he said and they were off, Papa running by Little Peter's side, holding the halter. The horse kept throwing up his head, trying to free himself from Papa's hand. He snorted and plunged so that Papa had all he could do not to be thrown off his feet and trampled. Hans was frightened and his head hurt. He bawled and struggled in Mama's arms. It was hard for her to hold him.

picketed (PIK-it-id) tied to a spike or stake in the ground

halter (HAWL-tor) ropes used for leading an animal

bawled (BAWLD) cried loudly

And just then Ilse, looking backwards, saw Baldy. The cow was trying to pull her picket chain loose, but she could not budge it. She was mooing and her eyes rolled. Ilse could not leave her there to die. Papa had always said that she must take care of Baldy.

"I'm getting Baldy," she called to Mama, as she slipped from Little Peter's back. But Mama, trying to quiet the struggling Hans and to keep her seat at the same time, never heard her, nor felt her hands loosen from her waist. Papa did not see her either.

Alone across the prairie Ilse ran. The black cloud towered above her like one of the wicked genie. Now below it she could see the red of running flames, and the howling of the wind was mixed with the cries of the birds flying before it. A big rabbit struck against her legs and nearly knocked her over, but she ran on.

By the time she had unfastened Baldy, it was too late to reach the river. They were cut off by a wall of fire. The sun was darkened, and ashes were blowing about them. But Ilse did not lose her head. She must get Baldy into the sod barn at least, and Baldy, too, was glad to seek shelter in the stall that had always meant safety to her.

Panting in the darkness of the windowless building, Ilse looked about. Only the door would burn. If she could wet it down, now! The spring was not far off.

She snatched a horse blanket from the peg on which it hung. There were no pails in the barn as the

genie (JEE-nee) magical spirits

sod (SAHD) soil and grass that has been taken off the ground

animals were taken to the spring to drink, but a wet blanket would not burn easily. Closing the door behind her to keep Baldy in, Ilse ran stumbling towards the spring. All about her tongues of flames, torn loose by the wind from the roaring fire which followed, were flying by her. The air was hard to breathe.

She reached the spring and wet the blanket. But now it weighed so much that she could scarcely drag it after her. Still, she did not give up easily. She was stumbling over the sod now, and the dry grass with which it bristled was catching fire here and there about her. The great wall of flame was rushing down upon her. Already it was splitting about and engulfing the barn as a fiery river might split about and engulf a boulder. The sod house, too, was surrounded by fire. She was lost.

But even now Ilse kept her head. The heavy wet blanket dragged at her arms, as though reminding her that it was there. It was her only hope. Spreading it out on the furrowed sod, she crawled under it, making herself as small as she could.

Then the roaring filled her ears, and a great something crawled over her across the wet blanket, making a sizzling sound, and in a moment had passed

engulfing (en-GULF-ing) flowing over
boulder (BOHL-dur) a large rock
furrowed (FUR-ohd) plowed

by. She heard the uproar of the fire racing on and on across the prairie, driven by the wind. Further and further off it sounded, and at last she dared lift up the steaming blanket. She was not hurt. All about her the ground lay black, with here and there a wisp of smoke curling up from it, or a feeble tongue of fire dying as she watched it. The grass and flowers were burned from the sod roofs of the house and barn, but the buildings were standing. Even the smoke-blackened windows in the house were not broken, but the doors were smouldering.

Now she could walk across the ashes. When Papa and Mama hurried back they found Ilse hard at work with the milking pail, throwing water against the house door. She had already put out the fire eating at the barn door. She looked black as a chimney sweep.

"Baldy's safe!" she called to them.

Papa and Mama did not scold Ilse for the fright she had given them when at the river they found that she was not with them. They listened to her story and knew how well she had done her duty.

"A miss is as good as a mile," said Papa. "The fire never came down into the river bottoms at all. Thanks to you and the fact that the doors were made of green wood and didn't catch fire easily, no harm has been done, except to the garden, and we can plant that again."

smouldering (SMOHL-dur-ing) burning without a flame

■ Talk About the Story

1. What problem did Ilse and her family have?

2. Why did Ilse leave her parents and brother on their way to the river?

3. What problem did Ilse have because the fire spread so quickly?

4. What did Ilse do to solve her problem?

5. What do you think is the turning point of the story?

6. How did Ilse's parents feel about what Ilse did?

■ Think About the Story

1. Describe how Ilse felt lying under the wet blanket with the fire sweeping over her.

2. How would the story be different if it was told from Baldy's point of view?

3. If this story were a play, do you think it would be easy to perform on a stage? Why or why not?

4. Could this story have happened in a crowded city? Why or why not?

■ Write About the Story

Ilse's troubles began with a prairie fire. If the fire had not started, there would not have been trouble. Write a list of fire safety rules for outdoors. Then write a list of rules for indoors.

Spotlight on

Elizabeth Coatsworth

Elizabeth Coatsworth wrote her first children's story to prove a point. She had been talking with a friend. They had disagreed about something. Elizabeth Coatsworth knew only one way to settle the argument— write a book. So she did. She has been writing children's books ever since.

Elizabeth Coatsworth's stories are a little like history. They take place long ago. They show people living very differently from the way we live today. For Elizabeth Coatsworth, though, the stories are not history at all. They are based on things she remembers as a child. Even her books about faraway places are based on her own experiences.

For Elizabeth Coatsworth, story ideas come easily. And why not? They come from her very own life!

Other Books by Elizabeth Coatsworth
Away Goes Sally   *The Bears on Hemlock Mountain*
The Wonderful Day   *The Courage of Sarah Noble*

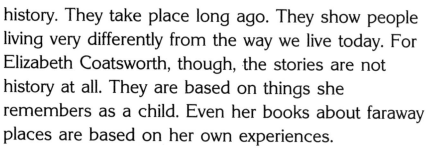

Eletelephony

by LAURA E. RICHARDS

Once there was an elephant,
Who tried to use the telephant-
No! No! I mean an elephone
Who tried to use the telephone-
(Dear me! I am not certain quite
That even now I've got it right.)

Howe'er it was, he got his trunk
Entangled in the telephunk;
The more he tried to get it free,
The louder buzzed the telephee-
(I fear I'd better drop the song
of elephop and telephong!)

Who has more trouble, the elephant or the poet?

As I Was Going Out One Day

As I was going out one day
My head fell off and rolled away.
But when I saw that it was gone,
I picked it up and put it on.

And when I got into the street
A fellow cried: "Look at your feet!"
I looked at them and sadly said:
"I've left them both asleep in bed!"

ANONYMOUS

What is silly about this poem?

Ilse's good sense helped her handle some serious troubles wisely. In "The Six Wise Travelers," some travelers also have troubles to handle. See if they handle their troubles wisely.

The Six Wise Travelers

by SALLY JARVIS

Players

SIX TRAVELERS
BOY

(Six wise travelers have come to the edge of a river.)

1ST TRAVELER: Oh, look, friends. We have come to a river. How will we get across?

2ND TRAVELER: I see a boy with a boat. We will ask him to take us.

3RD TRAVELER: Boy! Boy! Will you take us across the river in your boat?

BOY: There are too many of you for my little boat.

4TH TRAVELER: Silly boy! We are wiser than you. Let us use your boat.

BOY: Very well. But I will not go with you.

5TH TRAVELER: Let us go, travelers!

(They put the boat in the river.)

6TH TRAVELER: Ready? Everybody in! *(The six wise travelers get in the boat. The boat sinks.)*

1ST TRAVELER: Swim! Swim! Get to land! *(The six travelers swim to land.)*

2ND TRAVELER: Now I will count us to see that we are all here. *(He touches each man on the head as he counts.)* One, two, three, four, five. *(He does not count himself.)* OH! OH! One of us is missing!

3RD TRAVELER: Silly! You are counting wrong. Let me do it. *(He touches each man on the hand as he counts. He counts two hands for each man.)* One, two, three, four, five, six, seven, eight, nine, ten. Why, there are ten of us! That is why the boat sank!

4TH TRAVELER: Oh, you silly man. You counted two hands for each man. Let me do it. *(He touches each man on the back as he counts.)* One, two, three, four, five. *(He does not count himself.)* You are right! One traveler is missing! We will have to find him.

5TH TRAVELER: *(He sees the boy.)* Boy! Go and find the missing traveler!

6TH TRAVELER: We will give you a bag of gold if you find him.

BOY: Very well. Let me count you all first. One, two, three, four, five, six. *(Of course he counts them all.)* You are all here. I have found the missing man.

ALL SIX TRAVELERS: What a good boy! Here is your gold. When you grow up, maybe you will be as wise as we are. *(The six wise travelers jump in the river and swim to the other side.)*

■ Talk About the Story

1. What was the first problem that the travelers had?
2. What happened when the travelers tried to cross the river?
3. What did the travelers do after they reached the shore?
4. How did the boy earn the bag of gold?
5. Who was wiser, the boy or the travelers? Why do you think so?

■ Think About the Story

1. If you were the boy in the play, what would you think of the six wise travelers?
2. Why did the six wise travelers swim across the river at the end?
3. How else could the play have ended?
4. What do you think the six wise travelers would have done if the boy had not come along?

■ Write About the Story

The six wise travelers end up swimming across the river. Write a short play about what they would say and do after they reached the other side. Use what you already know about the travelers to help you figure out what to write.

Understanding Setting

■ Reading About Setting

The events in a story take place somewhere. Perhaps that somewhere is a town or a city like yours. Or, perhaps it is a fantasy land created by the author. The place where story events happen is part of the setting of a story.

The time in which story events happen is also part of the setting.

How might stories of long ago be different from stories set in the future? How can knowing about the setting of a story help you understand the story?

■ Thinking About Setting

The pictures that go with a story often contain clues about the setting of the story. Study these story pictures. Decide what each picture tells about the setting of the story.

From the picture on the left, you can figure out that the story takes place in a city. From the picture on the right, you can learn that the story takes place sometime in the future. The characters' dress and their way of traveling are clues to the time of story events.

■ Using What You Have Learned

Story sentences also have clues about the setting of the story. Read these sentences from "The Sod House." Then answer the questions.

Day after peaceful day went by. They saw nothing of their neighbors, except for some thin line of smoke from a far-off chimney, or a passing wagon or a rider trotting by.

The sun was darkened, and ashes were blowing about them. But Ilse did not lose her head. She must get Baldy into the sod barn at least, and Baldy, too, was glad to seek shelter in the stall that had always meant safety to her.

Which story sentences have clues to the setting of the story?

What are the clues? How do the clues help you figure out the setting of the story?

As you read, be on the look-out for clues to the setting of the story.

The six wise travelers had some troubles because they were really more foolish than wise. In "The Magic Fish" you will discover still other ways to find troubles.

The Magic Fish

by FREYA LITTLEDALE

Once upon a time there was a poor fisherman. He lived with his wife in an old hut by the sea. Every day he went fishing. One day the fisherman felt something on the end of his line. He pulled and he pulled. And up came a big fish.

That night his wife asked him, "Why didn't you catch any fish today?"

"I did catch a fish," said the man. "But he was a magic fish. He said he was really a prince. So I let him go."

"Silly man!" said his wife. "Why didn't you make a wish? Go back to the fish. Tell him I wish for a pretty house."

"Why?" asked the man.

"Never mind why," said his wife. "Go back and tell the fish I want a pretty house."

"I don't want to go," said the man.

"Go," said his wife.

So the fisherman went back to the sea.
The fisherman called,

"Oh, fish in the sea
come listen to me.
My wife begs a wish
from the magic fish."

"What does she want?" asked the fish.

"She wants a pretty house," said the man.

"Go home," the fish said. "Now your wife has a pretty house."

So the man went home. The old hut was gone.
Now there was a pretty house.

"This is very nice," the fisherman said to his wife.
"We will be happy here."

"We shall see," said his wife.

The fisherman was happy. His wife was happy, too.
She was happy for one week.

Then she said to the man, "Go back to the fish.
Tell him I want more than a pretty house. I want to
live in a castle."

"Why?" asked the man.

"Never mind why," said the woman. "Go back and
tell the fish I want a castle."

"But I don't want to go," said the man.

"Go," said his wife.

So the man went back to the sea. The man called,

"Oh, fish in the sea
Come listen to me.
My wife begs a wish
From the magic fish."

"Well," asked the fish. "What does she want now?"

"She wants a castle," said the man.

"Go home," the fish said. "Now your wife has a castle."

So the man went home. The pretty house was gone. And there was a castle.

"This is a beautiful castle," said the fisherman to his wife. "We will be happy here."

"We shall see," said his wife.

The fisherman was happy. And his wife was happy, too. She was happy for two weeks.

Then she said to the fisherman, "Go back to the fish. Tell him I want more than the castle. Tell him I want to be Queen of the land."

"Why?" asked the fisherman.

"Never mind why," said the woman. "Go back to the fish and tell him I must be Queen of the land."

"I don't want to go," said the fisherman.

"Go," said his wife.

So the man went back to the sea. The man called,

"Oh, fish in the sea
Come listen to me.
My wife begs a wish
From the magic fish."

"Well," said the fish, "What does she want this time?"

"She wants to be Queen of the land," said the man.

"Go home," said the fish. "Now your wife is Queen of the land."

So the fisherman went home. His wife was in the castle. She was sitting on a throne made of gold. And she wore a dress of gold and a crown made of gold.

"So," said the man, "Now you are Queen of the land. That is a fine thing to be. At last we can be happy."

"We shall see," said the wife.

And the fisherman was happy. His wife was happy, too. She was happy for three weeks.

Then she said to the fisherman, "Go back to the fish. Tell him I want to be more than Queen of the land. Tell him I want to be Queen of the sun and the moon and the stars."

"But why?" asked the fisherman.

"Never mind why," she said. "Just go back to the fish. Tell him I want to be Queen of the sun and the moon and the stars."

"I don't want to go," said the man. "The fish will be angry."

"Go," said his wife.

So the man went back to the sea. He called,

"Oh, fish in the sea
Come listen to me.
My wife begs a wish
From the magic fish."

"She wants to be Queen of the sun and the moon and the stars," said the fisherman.

"NO," said the fish. "She wants too much. She cannot be Queen of the sun. She cannot be Queen of the moon and the stars. Now she must go back to the old hut."

So the fisherman went home. The castle was gone. The old hut was back. And his wife was inside.

And there they are to this very day.

■ Talk About the Story

1. What special power did the magic fish have?

2. What did the fisherman's wife want?

3. At the end of the story, what happened to the fisherman and his wife? Why?

4. Should the magic fish have treated both the fisherman and his wife the same way? Why or why not?

5. Which of the characters in the story had troubles?

■ Think About the Story

1. How would the story be different if it were told from the wife's point of view?

2. What words would you use to describe the fisherman? His wife?

3. How do you think the fish became magical in the first place?

4. What do you think would have happened if the fisherman and his wife could have had as many wishes as they wanted?

■ Write About the Story

Imagine that you have caught a magic fish. Think about the wish you would ask the fish to grant. Write a paragraph about your wish. Tell what the wish is and why you would ask for it.

At the Library

The trouble with reading is, once you start it's hard to stop. If you would like to read more plays and stories like the ones in this unit, look for these books in your school library.

1. **Little Plays for Little People,** published by Parents' Magazine Press in 1965.

2. **The Magic Fish,** by Freya Littledale. Published by Scholastic in 1967.

3. **The Sod House,** by Elizabeth Coatsworth. Published by the Macmillan Publishing Company in 1954.

Tricks

Here are some stories of tricksters and tricks. Of monkeys and mothers and children who fix the problems they have with a bold, clever mix of courage and cunning and secrets and tricks.

See if you can figure out the trickiest trickster's trick of all tricks.

A trick is only as good as the trickster, but Kima, an east African monkey, is no trickster at all. Yet he finds himself in a spot where he must play the trick of a lifetime.

The Monkey's Heart

by ELEANOR B. HEADY

There once was a monkey called Kima who lived beside the sea in a great mbuyu tree. The branches of this tree were so wide that they hung far out over the water. On the tree grew the mbuyu fruit of which Kima was very <u>fond</u>.

Beneath the spreading branches of the mbuyu tree, in the warm blue water near the shore, lived Papa, the shark. Day after day he watched the monkey eating the fruit. Then one day Papa said to the monkey, "Please won't you throw some down to me?"

"Who is it?" asked Kima.

"I am Papa, the shark. I come every day to lie in the warm water near the shore. I'd like to taste that fruit. It looks delicious."

"It is. Here, catch this one," and Kima dropped a large fruit to the shark.

"Asante," said Papa. "It tastes delicious."

---

fond (FAHND) to like very much

So that is how Kima, the monkey, and Papa, the shark, became friends. Each day the shark came to the warm shore beneath the mbuyu tree. Kima dropped fruit to him and they ate and talked together. Each evening Papa returned to his home in the deep water of the sea.

One day when the shark appeared beneath the tree, he called to the monkey, "Kima, my friend, won't you come to my house to dine today?"

"I'd like to come, Papa, but can't go into the water. I don't know how to swim and would surely drown."

"I know you can't swim," said the shark. "Don't worry about that. You may ride on my back."

The monkey came down from the tree. The shark swam very close to shore. Kima climbed upon his back and they started out to sea. When they had gone only a short distance, Papa said, "I have something to tell you, something I hate to say."

"What is it?" asked Kima.

"I have tricked you. It is all my fault because I told my people of our friendship."

"What do you mean, Papa?"

"I was sent to get you, Kima. Our chief is very ill. The great medicine man said that only a monkey's heart will cure him."

"What?" gasped Kima.

"They made me come," insisted Papa. "I do not wish you harm."

"You've made a mistake, my friend," said Kima. "Haven't you heard that a monkey never takes his heart with him when he travels from home? Mine is back in the mbuyu tree where I live."

"In that case, we must go back to get it," said the shark.

"We must go back," agreed Kima. "It would never do for you to return home without it."

The huge fish turned around and carried the monkey back to his tree on the shore. Kima caught hold of a low-hanging branch and swung himself into the tree. He disappeared among the thick branches.

After a long silence, Papa called, "Haven't you found your heart?"

There was no answer.

The shark waited, then called again, "Why does it take you so long, Kima?"

Still there was only silence.

At last Papa called in a very loud voice, "Kima are you there? Have you no ears?"

Then from the green branches of the mbuyu tree came the monkey's answer. "For those who would betray my friendship I have neither heart nor ears."

---

betray (bee-TRAY) to be disloyal or false

■ Talk About the Story

1. Who are the two friends in the story?
2. Papa solved his problem and at the same time, created a problem for Kima. What was Kima's problem?
3. How did Kima solve his problem?
4. Why do you think Papa told Kima about what was going to happen when they reached home? Would you have done the same thing? Why or why not?
5. How do you think Papa felt after he found out that he had been tricked?
6. Why was Kima's trick the trick of a lifetime?

■ Think About the Story

1. How do you think Papa felt when he had to choose between saving his chief and betraying his friend Kima?
2. Do you think Kima would ever forgive Papa?
3. What do you think Kima would do if another shark tried to make friends with him?
4. Kima says that monkey's always leave their hearts at home. What do you always leave at home when you go out?
5. Suppose Papa had taken Kima to his house. How might Kima escape then?

■ Write About the Story

At the end of the story, Papa did not have the monkey's heart he needed to help cure the chief. What do you think Papa should do? Explain your ideas in a paragraph. Tell what Papa should do and why he should do it.

Enjoying Folk Literature

Before there was television, or books, or record players, people entertained themselves and others by telling stories. The stories they told were not written down anywhere. The storytellers just remembered them from having heard them before. As the stories were told over and over again, details often changed, but the main ideas stayed the same.

Over time, many of these stories were written down. Today we can enjoy reading them as folktales.

Think about the folktale you have just read, "The Monkey's Heart." Retell the story in your own words. Which details changed when you retold the story? Which stayed the same?

As you read the next folktale, decide if the main ideas of the story are like others you already know about.

The Gingerbread Man

by ROWENA BENNETT

The gingerbread man gave a gingery shout:
"Quick! Open the oven and let me out!"
He stood up straight in his baking pan.
He jumped to the floor and away he ran.
"Catch me," he called, "if you can, can, can."

The gingerbread man met a cock and a pig
And a dog that was brown and twice as big
As himself. But he called to them all as he ran,
"You can't catch a runaway gingerbread man."

The gingerbread man met a reaper and sower.
The gingerbread man met a thresher and
    mower;
But no matter how fast they scampered and ran
They couldn't catch up with the gingerbread
    man.

Then he came to a fox and he turned to face
    him.
He dared Old Reynard to follow and chase him;
But when he stepped under the fox's nose
Something happened. What do you s'pose?
The fox gave a snap. The fox gave a yawn,
And the gingerbread man was gone, gone,
    GONE.

What happened to the gingerbread man?

89

Prickled Pickles
Don't Smile

by NIKKI GIOVANNI

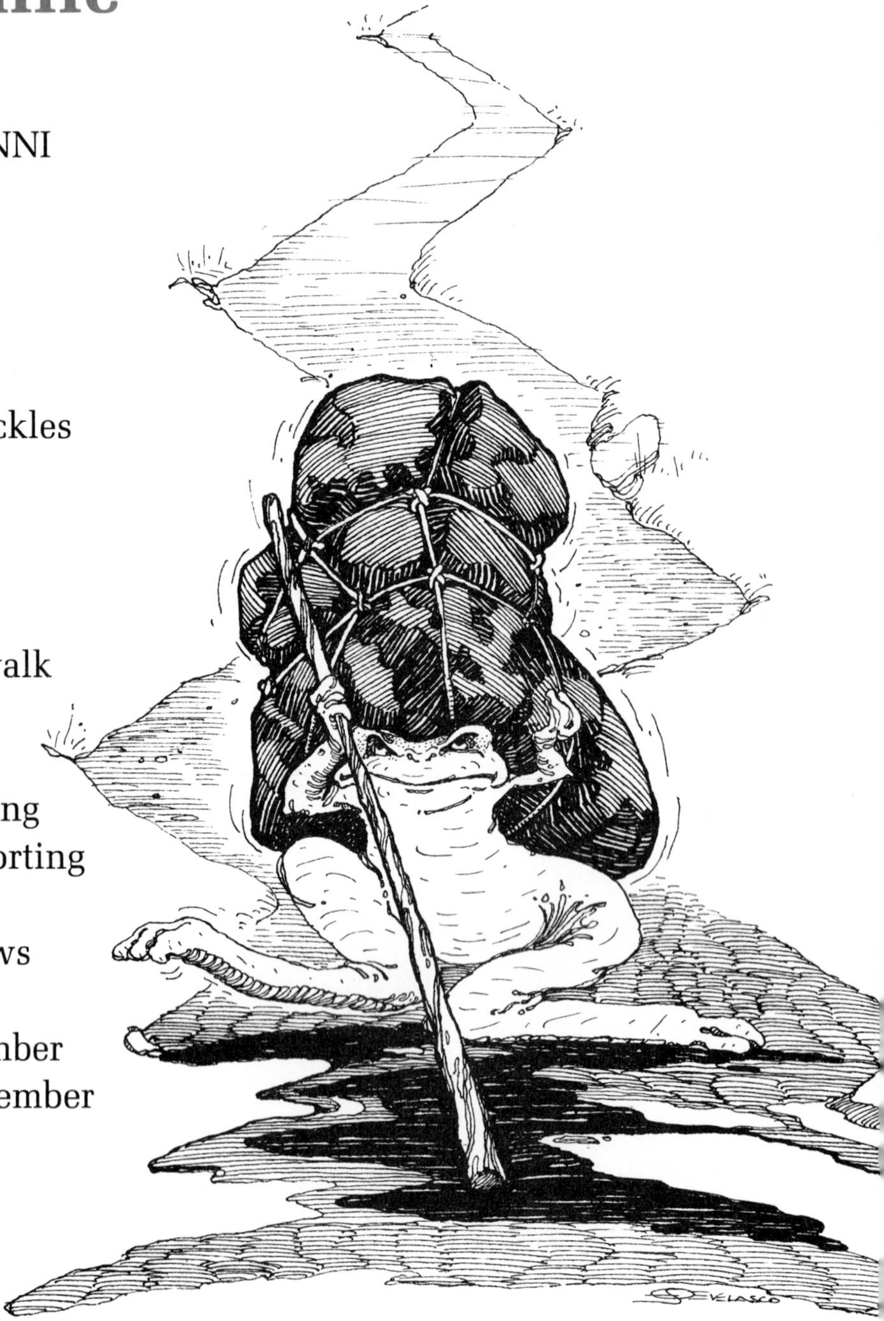

Never tickle
a prickled pickle
cause prickled pickles
Don't smile

Never goad
a loaded toad
when he has to walk
A whole mile

Froggies go courting
with weather reporting
that indicates
There are no snows

But always remember
the month of December
is very hard
On your nose

Which part of this poem makes you smile?

Kima had to trick Papa in order to save his own life. In "The First Day of School," Ramona must figure out another way to out-trick a trickster.

The First Day of School

by BEVERLY CLEARY

Ramona Quimby hoped her parents would forget to give her a little talking-to. She did not want anything to spoil this exciting day.

"Ha-ha, I get to ride the bus to school all by myself," Ramona bragged to her big sister, Beatrice, at breakfast. Her stomach felt quivery with excitement at the day ahead, a day that would begin with a bus ride just the right length to make her feel a long way from home but not long enough—she hoped—to make her feel carsick.

After the family's rush to brush teeth, Mr. Quimby said to his daughters, "Hold out your hands," and into each waiting pair he dropped a new pink eraser. "Just for luck," he said, "not because I expect you to make mistakes."

"Thank you," said the girls. Even a small present was appreciated, because presents of any kind had been scarce while the family tried to save money so Mr. Quimby could return to school. Ramona, who liked to draw as much as her father, especially treasured the new eraser, smooth, pearly pink, smelling softly of rubber, and just right for erasing pencil lines.

Mrs. Quimby handed each member of her family a lunch, two in paper bags and one in a lunch box for Ramona. "Now, Ramona—" she began.

Ramona sighed. Here it was, that little talking-to she always <u>dreaded</u>.

"Please remember," said her mother, "you really must be nice to Willa Jean."

Ramona made a face. "I try, but it's awfully hard."

<u>dreaded</u> (DRED-id) didn't want to face

Being nice to Willa Jean was the part of Ramona's life she wished would change. Every day after school she had to go to her friend Howie Kemp's house, where her parents paid Howie's grandmother to look after her until one of them could come for her. Both of Howie's parents, too, went off to work each day. She liked Howie, but after spending most of the summer, except for swimming lessons in the park, at the Kemps' house, she was tired of having to play with four-year-old Willa Jean. She was also tired of apple juice and graham crackers for a snack every single day.

"No matter what Willa Jean does," complained Ramona, "her grandmother thinks it's my fault because I'm bigger."

Mrs. Quimby gave Ramona a quick hug. "I know it isn't easy, but keep trying."

When Ramona sighed, her father hugged her and said, "Remember, kid, we're counting on you." Then he began to sing, "We've got high hopes, try hopes, buy cherry pie-in July hopes—"

Ramona enjoyed her father's making up new words for the song about the little old ant moving the rubber tree plant, and she liked being big enough to be counted on, but sometimes when she went to the Kemps' she felt as if everything depended on her. If Howie's grandmother did not look after her, her mother could not work full time. If her mother did not work full time, her father could not go to school. If her father did not go to school, he might have to go back to being a checker, the work that made him tired and cross.

Still, Ramona had too many interesting things to

think about to let her responsibility worry her as she walked through the autumn sunshine toward her school bus stop, her new eraser in hand, new sandals on her feet, that quivery feeling of excitement in her stomach, and the song about high hopes running through her head.

When Ramona reached the bus stop, she found Howie Kemp already waiting with his grandmother and Willa Jean, who had come to wave good-by.

The bus, the little yellow school bus Ramona had waited all summer to ride, pulled up at the curb. Ramona and Howie climbed aboard as if they were used to getting on buses by themselves. I did it just like a grown-up, thought Ramona.

"Good morning. I am Mrs. Hanna, your bus aide," said a woman sitting behind the driver. "Take the first empty seats toward the back."

As soon as the bus pulled away from the curb, Ramona felt someone kick the back of her seat. She

turned and faced a sturdy boy wearing a baseball cap with the visor turned up and a white T-shirt with a long word printed across the front. Ramona faced front without speaking. This boy was not going to spoil her first day in the third grade.

Thump, thump, thump against the back of Ramona's seat. The bus stopped for other children, some excited and some anxious. Still the kicking continued. Ramona ignored it as the bus passed her former school. Good old Glenwood, thought Ramona, as if she had gone there a long, long time ago.

"All right, Danny," said the bus aide to the kicking boy. "As long as I'm riding shotgun on this bus, we won't have anyone kicking the seats. Understand?"

Ramona smiled to herself as she heard Danny mutter an answer. How funny—the bus aide saying she was riding shotgun as if she were guarding a

---

ignore (ig-NOR) pay no attention to

former (FOR-mer) the one before

shipment of gold on a stagecoach instead of making children behave on a little yellow school bus.

Ramona pretended she was riding a stagecoach pursued by robbers until she discovered her eraser, her beautiful pink eraser, was missing. "Did you see my eraser?" she asked a second-grade girl, who had taken the seat beside her. The two searched the seat and the floor. No eraser.

Ramona felt a tap on her shoulder and turned. "Was it a pink eraser?" asked the boy in the baseball cap.

"Yes." Ramona was ready to forgive him for kicking her seat. "Have you seen it?"

"Nope." The boy grinned as he jerked down the visor of his baseball cap.

That grin was too much for Ramona. "Liar!" she said with her most ferocious glare, and faced front once more, angry at the loss of her new eraser, angry with herself for dropping it so the boy could find it.

The bus stopped at Cedarhurst, Ramona's new school, a two-story red-brick building very much like her old school. As the children hopped out of the bus, Ramona felt a little thrill of triumph. She had not been carsick. She now discovered she felt as if she had grown even more than her feet. Third-graders were the biggest people—except teachers, of course—at this school. All the little first- and second-graders running around the playground, looking so young, made Ramona feel tall, grown-up, and sort of . . . well, wise in the ways of the world.

---

pursued (per-SOOD) chased

ferocious (fer-OH-shus) fierce

96

Danny shoved ahead of her. "Catch!" he yelled to another boy. Something small and pink flew through the air and into the second boy's cupped hands. The boy wound up as if he were pitching a baseball, and the eraser flew back to Danny.

"You gimme back my eraser!" <u>Encumbered</u> by her lunch box, Ramona chased Danny, who ran, ducking and dodging, among the first- and second-graders. When she was about to catch him, he tossed her eraser to the other boy. If her lunch box had not banged against her knees, Ramona might have been able to grab him. Unfortunately, the bell rang first.

"Yard apes!" yelled Ramona, tears of anger in her eyes. "Yucky yard apes!" The boys, of course, paid no attention.

<u>encumbered</u> (en-CUM-berd) weighed down with

Still fuming, Ramona entered her new school and climbed the stairs to find her assigned classroom. Ramona's new room was filled with excitement and confusion. She saw some people she had known at her old school. Others were strangers. Everyone was talking at once, shouting greetings to old friends or looking over those who would soon become new friends, rivals, or enemies.

Ramona missed Howie, who had been assigned to another room, but wouldn't you know? That yard ape, Danny, was sitting at a desk, still wearing his baseball cap and tossing Ramona's new eraser from one hand to another. Ramona was too frustrated to speak. She wanted to hit him. How dare he spoil her day!

"My name is Mrs. Whaley," said the teacher, as she printed her name on the blackboard. "W-h-a-l-e-y. I'm a whale with a y for a tail." She laughed and so did her class. Then the whale with a y for a tail handed Ramona some slips of paper. "Please pass these out," she directed. "We need some name tags until I get to know you."

Ramona did as she was told, and as she walked among the desks she discovered her new sandals squeaked. Squeak, creak, squeak. Ramona giggled, and so did the rest of the class. Squeak, creak, squeak. Ramona went up one aisle and down the other. The last person she gave a slip to was the boy from the bus, who was still wearing his baseball cap. "You give me back my eraser, you yard ape!" she whispered.

"Try and get it, Bigfoot," he whispered back with a grin.

---

fuming (FYOOM-ing) very angry

98

Ramona stared at her feet, Bigfoot? Bigfoot was a hairy creature ten feet tall, who was supposed to leave huge footprints in the mountain snows of southern Oregon. Some people thought they had seen Bigfoot slipping through the forests, but no one had ever been able to prove he really existed.

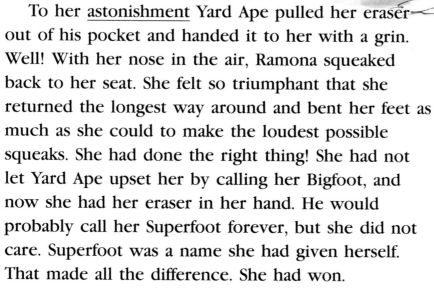

Bigfoot indeed! Ramona's feet had grown, but they were not huge. She was not going to let him get away with this insult. "Superfoot to you, Yard Ape," she said right out loud, realizing too late that she had given herself a new nickname.

To her <u>astonishment</u> Yard Ape pulled her eraser out of his pocket and handed it to her with a grin. Well! With her nose in the air, Ramona squeaked back to her seat. She felt so triumphant that she returned the longest way around and bent her feet as much as she could to make the loudest possible squeaks. She had done the right thing! She had not let Yard Ape upset her by calling her Bigfoot, and now she had her eraser in her hand. He would probably call her Superfoot forever, but she did not care. Superfoot was a name she had given herself. That made all the difference. She had won.

Ramona became aware that she was squeaking in the midst of an unusual silence. She stopped midsqueak when she saw her new teacher watching her with a little smile. The class was watching the teacher.

---

astonishment (as-TON-ish-ment) surprise

"We all know you have musical shoes," said Mrs. Whaley. Of course the class laughed.

By walking with stiff legs and not bending her feet, Ramona reached her seat without squeaking at all. She did not know what to think. At first she thought Mrs. Whaley's remark was a reprimand, but then maybe her teacher was just trying to be funny. She couldn't tell about grown-ups sometimes. Ramona finally decided that any teacher who would let Yard Ape wear his baseball cap in the classroom wasn't really fussy about squeaking shoes.

Ramona bent over her paper and wrote slowly and carefully in cursive, Ramona Quimby, age 8. She admired the look of what she had written, and she was happy. She liked feeling tall in her new school.

---

reprimand (REP-rih-mand) a scolding

She liked—or was pretty sure she liked—her nonfussy teacher. Yard Ape—Well, he was a problem, but so far she had not let him get the best of her for keeps. Besides, although she might never admit it to anyone, now that she had her eraser back she liked him—sort of. Maybe she enjoyed a challenge.

Ramona began to draw a fancy border, all scallops and curliques, around her name. She was happy, too, because her family had been happy that morning and because she was big enough for her family to depend on.

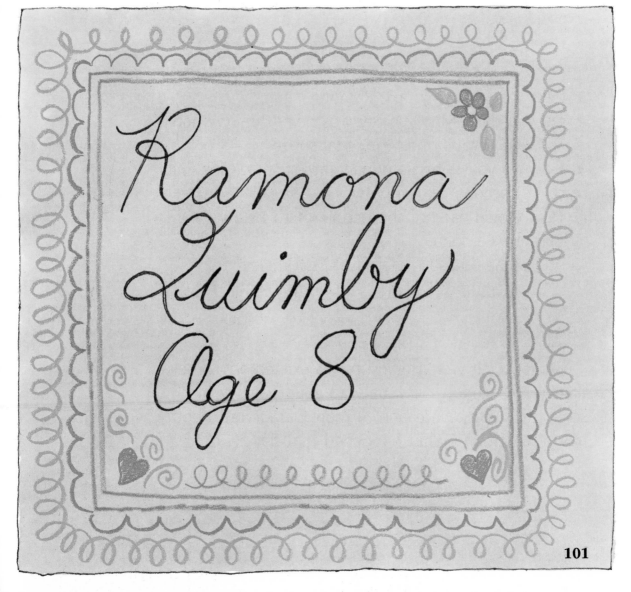

■ Talk About the Story

1. What is special about the day on which the story takes place?

2. What happened on the school bus that upset Ramona?

3. Why do you think Yard Ape finally gave back the eraser?

4. Which of these words describe the boy who Ramona called Yard Ape: cruel, a tease, friendly?

5. Was Ramona a shy person? How do you know? What did Ramona do that a shy person would not do?

■ Think About the Story

1. Why would Danny take Ramona's eraser?

2. Do you think Mrs. Whaley was being funny when she said Ramona had "musical shoes"?

3. How do you think Ramona's father felt on his first day of school? Explain why.

4. How would each of the people listed below describe Ramona?

Ramona's Mother	Mrs. Whaley
Ramona's Father	Danny

■ Write About the Story

Ramona felt very grown-up and excited about her first day of school. Think back to your first day of school this year. Write one or more paragraphs about how you felt and what happened that day.

Spotlight on

Beverly Cleary

When Beverly Cleary was young, she liked reading funny stories about other children. The problem was she couldn't find many of those kinds of stories in the library. That's when Beverly Cleary made a big decision. She would become a writer.

Beverly Cleary wrote her first story when she was in sixth grade. Her teacher encouraged her to keep on writing.

Encouragement was all Beverly Cleary needed. Nothing could stop her now, but first she had some things to do. She went to college. Afterward, she worked as a librarian. Then, one day she decided it was time to keep her promise to herself. *Henry Huggins,* her first book, was about the funny adventures of a third-grader.

Other Books by Beverly Cleary

Henry and Beezus   *Ramona the Pest*
Ellen Tebbits   *Mitch and Amy*

Ramona got what she wanted without using tricks. In "Alexandra the Rock-Eater," Alexandra can't possibly get what she wants without them.

Alexandra the Rock-Eater

by DOROTHY VAN WOERKOM

Long ago, near a dark forest, lived a man named Igor and his wife Alexandra. They had a fine house, a field of turnips, and a cow that gave two pails of milk every day.

They had trees full of fruit and hives full of honey—but not a single child to call their own.

One day as they worked in their field, Alexandra pulled up a turnip and said, "How I wish we had a child to share this turnip with us!"

Igor laughed. "Only one? I wish we had *two* children to share *two* turnips." And he tossed two large turnips into their cart.

"A dozen children for a dozen turnips!" Alexandra shouted, pulling up a dozen turnips.

"Dozens of dozens!" Igor cried.

And they tossed dozens of dozens of turnips into the cart.

When the cart was full, they pushed it up the hill to their house. Suddenly Igor stopped. "Look!" he said to Alexandra.

Alexandra looked. There were children in the yard. Children in the trees. Children spilling out of the house and the wood shed. Dozens and dozens of children running down the hill to meet them.

"Oh, my!" Alexandra cried. "How many are there? How many?"

Igor was counting, "—ninety-eight, ninety-nine, one hundred. We have a hundred children," he said, smiling. "And that is not *one* too many!"

Alexandra agreed with that, and she and Igor made room in their house for every single one of them.

But their hundred children soon ate all the turnips in the field and all the honey in the hives. And they drank milk until the cow was dry.

"Before we know it, all the fruit will be gone, too," said Alexandra finally. And off she went to find more food.

She walked to the far side of the forest. It was midnight. There she saw cows and sheep on a hill, and an old shepherd tending them.

Suddenly she saw a bright green light and heard a noise like the wind. From down the road came a young dragon. He snatched a ram, a sheep, a lamb, and three fine cows from the shepherd's flock and ran up the road again.

"Come back!" the shepherd shouted. But the dragon kept on going.

"Oh, my!" said Alexandra. "That was something to see!"

The shepherd sighed and said, "Every midnight that young dragon comes and snatches a ram, a sheep, a lamb, and three fine cows."

"Well now," said Alexandra, thinking of her hundred hungry children, "if I get rid of that dragon forever, what will you give me?"

"I will give you one of every three rams, one of every three sheep, one of every three lambs, and a cow every year for as long as you live," said the shepherd.

"Then I will do it!" Alexandra said.

She looked at the shepherd's soft round cheeses made from the milk of his fine cows. "First I will need one of those small cheeses and one of those large cheeses," she said and then added, "and also a good pocketknife."

"Help yourself," said the shepherd.

When the next midnight came, Alexandra stood in the middle of the road with the small round cheese at her feet and the large round cheese in her hand. At last she saw the green light and heard the noise like the wind.

"Stop!" she shouted.

"Dear me!" the young dragon said, "Who are you, and what are you doing in the middle of the road?"

"I am Alexandra the Rock-Eater," she said, taking a bite of the big cheese in her hand.

"And from small stones like this, I squeeze buttermilk." She picked up the small cheese and squeezed it so hard that milk came out. "If you snatch anything more from this poor shepherd's flock, I will squeeze you as small as a lizard!"

Now on the far side of a forest at midnight, two cheeses do look like a rock and a stone.

"Oh my!" said the dragon. "I wish I had you for a friend. Will you come home with me and meet my mother?"

"I have no time for dragons," Alexandra said. "Not with a hundred children to feed."

At first the young dragon looked sad, then he grinned. "If you will come home with me for three days, I will give you three sacks full of gold!"

"For three sacks full of gold I will come," Alexandra said. And she walked down the road with the dragon.

When they came to the dragon's cave, the mother dragon frowned fiercely and said, "Why do you bring home this weak two-legged thing instead of a ram, a sheep, a lamb, and three fine cows?"

"Listen, Momma," said the dragon. "This is Alexandra the Rock-Eater! She is so strong that she can squeeze buttermilk out of a stone! She has come to visit us for three days, for three sacks full of gold."

His mother snorted and rolled her red eyes. "You do find the most unusual creatures when you go out. Well, I suppose she can stay for three days," the mother dragon said with a sigh. "She is too small and puny to give us much trouble. Now sit down and eat your supper."

She poured soup into two dragon-size bowls. To Alexandra she gave a fiery glare and a dragon-size spoon full of soup.

The next day the young dragon took a club from the wall of the cave. Alexandra had never seen such a club. "Come outside with me," said the dragon. "Let's see who can throw this the farthest."

The young dragon swung the club around and around. Then he hurled it as hard as he could. It landed three miles away.

---

puny (PYOO-nee) weak
hurled (HERLD) threw

By the time they found it again, it was evening. Alexandra tried to lift the club. Not even with the help of Igor and their hundred children could she have lifted that club!

"If these dragons find out how weak I really am, they will surely eat me!" she thought. And then she had an idea.

"Go ahead!" cried the dragon. "What are you waiting for?"

"Can't you see?" Alexandra said. "The moon is in my way. Do you want me to hit it and put out its light?"

"Put out the moon!" yelled the dragon. "That would be terrible! We hunt by the light of the moon. I'll tell you what! Let me throw the club again, instead of you. Then the moon will be safe."

"No, I want my turn," Alexandra said. "Just wait till the moon moves a speck to the right."

But the dragon begged, "I will give you seven sacks full of gold!"

"For seven sacks full of gold, you can throw the club again," Alexandra said. And the dragon threw the club another three miles.

"Dear me!" he said to his mother that night. "Would you think that Alexandra the Rock-Eater could throw this club right onto the moon?"

His mother blew smoke through her nose. "I wish you had left that two-legged thing where you found her," she said.

The next day the young dragon said to Alexandra, "Today we must work. My Momma wants us to bring her some water." He picked up two pails and ran down to the river to fill them.

Alexandra had never seen such huge pails! She followed the dragon, watching him fill the pails and carry them home.

"Now these dragons will surely find me out and eat me!" she thought. Then she remembered the knife in her pocket. She knelt down and started to dig.

The dragon returned with the two empty pails.

"Now what are you doing?" he grumbled. "You had better hurry and take your turn. My Momma needs lots of water today."

"Well, that is a silly way to get it," Alexandra said. "I will just dig up the river and bring all the water to your Momma at once."

"Dig up the river!" yelled the dragon. "Then where would we go to swim? That would never do! I'll tell you what! I'll take your turn with the pails."

"Don't bother," said Alexandra, and she dug some more with the knife.

The dragon began to worry. "I'll give you seven *more* sacks full of gold," he said.

"For seven more sacks full of gold, you can take my turn with the pails," Alexandra told him.

So the young dragon carried the pails back and forth for the rest of the day.

On the third day the young dragon said, "Today we must go to the forest. My Momma needs wood for the fire."

When they came to the forest, the dragon began pulling up trees. Poor Alexandra knew that her knife would not help her now.

"Why are you standing there?" the young dragon shouted. "Pull up some trees."

Alexandra caught sight of a long vine. She began winding it around the tree trunks.

"Oh, now what?" snapped the dragon.

"It is silly to bring a few <u>meager</u> trees to your Momma," Alexandra said, weaving the vine around and around. "When I pull on this vine, they will *all* fall down. I will bring back the whole forest at once."

<u>meager</u> (MEE-ger) small

112

"Bring the whole forest!" the young dragon screamed. "But then where would I hide when my Momma gets angry with me? That would be the worst of all! I'll tell you what! Please let me carry the wood, and I'll give you seven times seven *more* sacks full of gold."

"All right, all right, for seven times seven more sacks full of gold, you can carry the wood," Alexandra said.

So the young dragon carried wood home till the sun went down.

That night he said to his mother, "Dear me! Alexandra the Rock-Eater is no fun at all. I'm glad she's going home tomorrow. Momma, she is stronger than even *Grandfather* was—and I've promised her sixty-six bags full of gold!"

"Listen to me," said his mother. "Gold is not that easy to come by. And what will we do if this creature comes back with her two-legged friends to take more from us? Tonight while she sleeps you must give her a whack on the head with your club."

But Alexandra had her ear to the wall of the cave, and she heard the plan. That night she filled a bag with sand and put it under her blanket. She said good night to the dragons, crawled under the bed, and lay very still.

The young dragon soon came tiptoeing in, with his

tail tiptailing behind. He raised the club high and struck the bed with a mighty blow.

From under the bed came Alexandra's mightiest groan. That was enough for the dragon. He yawned a wide yawn and went back to bed.

The next day at breakfast, the dragons were telling each other how clever they were when they heard Alexandra say, "Good morning."

The surprised mother dragon's spoon went clattering onto the floor. "Why, good morning," she said with a bewildered snort. "Did you sleep well?"

"Well enough," Alexandra said. "But once in the night, a pesky old flea flew into my room and bit me."

"A flea!" the young dragon shouted.

His mother jumped up and began bustling about the cave, throwing handfuls of gold into sacks. "Here," she said. "Here. And here. All this is yours if you leave right away and never return!"

But Alexandra knew she could not lift even one of those sacks.

"WHY DON'T YOU GO?" the young dragon screamed. "WHAT MORE COULD YOU POSSIBLY WANT?"

"I think I should stay for another three days," Alexandra said. "If I go home with just these few sacks full of gold, my husband will say I have no more sense than a dragon."

"Dear me!" the mother dragon shrieked. "Take seven times the number of these sacks. Or even seven times seven! Just leave!"

"Seven times seven will do," Alexandra said. "And I'll tell you what. Have your son carry these sacks, so my husband can't say that I am as weak as a dragon."

The young dragon sighed. Even the spaces between his teeth ached from his three days' hard work. But he picked up the sacks full of gold and followed Alexandra.

When they came to the road near her house, they saw a hundred children sitting on benches at long tables under the trees. Igor was dishing the last of the fruit into bowls.

"Oh, look!" cried one of the children. "Momma is here with a dragon! We will have dragon for supper tonight!"

Then all the children came running. The poor dragon saw, in a hundred right hands, a hundred sharp knives. He saw, in a hundred left hands, a hundred long forks. He dropped the sacks full of gold and ran.

When the shepherd on the hill saw him running away, he laughed and called out, "Goodbye, young dragon! Goodbye forever!"

"Goodbye, Alexandra the Rock-Eater!" the young dragon shouted. "Goodbye FOREVER!"

And the shepherd gave Alexandra one of every three rams, one of every three sheep, one of every three lambs, and a cow every year for as long as she lived.

■ Talk About the Story

1. What problem did Alexandra and Igor have because they had so many children?

2. What problem did the shepherd have?

3. How did Alexandra and the shepherd decide to work together to help solve their different problems?

4. What did Alexandra do to get rid of the dragon?

5. Which of these words describe Alexandra: foolish, brave, clever, strong, lazy? Explain your answer.

6. What do you think the dragon might have done if he had caught on to Alexandra's trick? How might the story be different?

7. Which of Alexandra's tricks did you like best? Why?

■ Think About the Story

1. Describe the dragon's cave in your own words.

2. How would you describe the young dragon? Why?

3. Do you think Alexandra could have tricked the mother dragon as easily as she tricked the young dragon? Why or why not?

4. What could Alexandra and her husband have done to feed the children if she had not seen the dragon?

■ Write About the Story

Imagine that Alexandra had stayed with the dragon family one more day. What act of strength might the dragons want her to perform? How would she trick the dragons into thinking she could do it? Write two paragraphs explaining your ideas.

Understanding Story Characters

■ Reading About Story Characters

Imagine that you had a chore that you didn't want to do. Would you try to trick someone else into doing it for you? Would you try to bully someone into doing it? Or would you do it yourself even though you didn't want to? What you did to solve your problem would tell something about the kind of person you were.

Story characters are like people. They have problems to solve and goals to reach. Like people, different characters have different ways of trying to get what they need. The things story characters do to get what they need tell something about the kinds of characters they are.

■ Thinking About Story Characters

Below is a list of some things the young dragon in "Alexandra the Rock-Eater" did. Use this information to decide how best to describe the dragon.

1. The dragon did not look carefully at Alexandra's rocks to see that they were really cheese.
2. The dragon believed everything Alexandra said about her strength and what she could do.
3. The dragon did not ask Alexandra to prove her strength.

You might describe the dragon as friendly, but foolish. He was friendly in asking Alexandra to visit him, but foolish in believing everything she said.

■ Using What You Have Learned

Read this cartoon. Think about what the characters do. Then answer the questions.

Which word best describes the younger daughter?
        wise   careful   foolish   cruel
Which word best describes the mother?
        wise   careful   foolish   cruel
What did each character do that helped you decide on the best describing word?

Think about what the characters do. In the next story use this information to figure out what kind of characters they are.

Alexandra figured out how to trick the dragon family and get what she needed. In "The Bird of Seven Colors," a young girl gets some tricky help from a mother.

The Bird of Seven Colors

by RICARDO E. ALEGRIA

There was a mother who had two daughters. The <u>elder</u>, who <u>resembled</u> her mother, she loved very much, but she did not care for the younger daughter. One day she sent the younger daughter to the fountain for water, and on the way the girl dropped the water pitcher and it broke. The mother was furious. To punish her daughter, she sent her from home to look for the Bird of Seven Colors who would mend the pitcher, and she told her daughter that she could not come home again until the pitcher was mended.

<u>elder</u> (EL-der) older

<u>resembled</u> (ree-ZEM-bld) looked like

120

The unhappy girl set out without knowing which way to go to find the Bird of Seven Colors. As she passed a mango tree, it spoke to her and asked where she was going. She said she was looking for the Bird of Seven Colors.

The tree said, "When you find him, ask him why I, who am so big and leafy, give no fruit."

The girl promised that she would and continued walking until she came to the seashore.

When the sea saw her, it asked where she was going, and she told it she was going in search of the Bird of Seven Colors.

The sea said, "When you find him, ask him why my waters, so <u>vast</u> and deep, hold no fish."

The girl promised she would, then she went on until she reached the King's house. The King's daughters asked her where she was going, and she told them her story. They asked her, if she found the Bird of Seven Colors, to ask him why they, being so beautiful, had no children. The girl promised she would, and went on her way in search of the bird.

Finally, she reached an enchanted mountain where the Bird of Seven Colors lived with the little old woman who was his mother. When the mother of the Bird of Seven Colors saw the girl, she asked what she was doing there, and the girl told her story again. The little old woman said that she would help her, but that she must hide, for her son was wicked, and if he saw her there he would eat her. So that the Bird of Seven Colors would not see the girl when he came home, his mother hid her in a barrel.

---

vast (VAST) very large

It wasn't long before the Bird of Seven Colors arrived. When the bird was in bed, the mother called, "Birdling! Birdling!" and the bird asked what she wanted. She said that she had broken a pitcher and wondered if he could fix it. He did, in no time at all, and went back to bed. It wasn't long before the mother called again. "Birdling! Birdling!"

He woke up and asked, "What is the matter, Mother?" The little old woman said that she had been dreaming about a very great mango tree with luxuriant foliage, that bore no fruit. The Bird of Seven Colors told her that was because there was a treasure buried among its roots and until the treasure was dug up, the tree would bear no fruit. The girl heard everything from her hiding place in the barrel. She rejoiced at having the answer to the mango tree's question.

Again the little old woman called, "Birdling! Birdling!" The bird woke up and asked what she wanted. The old woman asked why a great, deep sea might not have fish in its waters.

The bird grumbled sleepily, "It has to swallow someone before it can have fish." and went back to sleep.

It wasn't long before the old woman called again. "Birdling! Birdling!" The Bird of Seven Colors grew furious. He sat up in bed and told her that if she didn't let him sleep he would eat her! The little old woman said that she had been dreaming about the King's daughters who were very beautiful but had no children.

---

foliage (FOH-lee-ij) leaves
rejoiced (re-JOIST) felt joy

The angry bird snapped at his mother. "They'll have no children until they stop gazing at the moon!" and he went back to sleep.

The girl was overjoyed. Now her pitcher was mended and she knew the answers to the questions that had been asked her. In the morning, after the Bird of Seven Colors left, the little old woman took her out of the barrel. She gave her something to eat and said, "Now that you have what you came for, go, before my son returns!"

The grateful girl kissed the little old woman who had done so much for her and went home along the road by which she had come. When she reached the King's house, his daughters asked her if she had the answer to their question. "Yes. I have," she answered. And she told them what the Bird of Seven Colors had said. The King's daughters were so pleased that they gave her many pretty clothes and pieces of jewelry. When she came to the sea, it asked her if she had the

answer to its question. "Yes, I have. Wait a minute, and I'll tell you," and she turned around and walked far, far from the shore. Then she called back, "The Bird of Seven Colors says that in order to have fish, you must swallow someone." Then she ran away as fast as she could for she knew that the sea is <u>treacherous</u> and would try to swallow her. The sea reached out a great, long wave, trying to catch her, but she was too far away.

After walking a long time, the girl reached the mango tree and told it what the Bird of Seven Colors had said. Then the tree begged her to dig at its roots and remove the treasure. She did, and she found enough gold coins to fill her pitcher.

After she left the tree it did not take her long to reach home. Her mother was very surprised when she saw her dressed in pretty clothes and even more surprised when she saw the mended pitcher filled with gold coins. The girl told her everything. Immediately, the vain woman set out for the house of the Bird of Seven Colors to see if there was another treasure hidden somewhere. She was thinking so hard about the riches she would find that she forgot what her daughter had said about the sea, and as she passed by on the shore, it reached out a great, long wave, pulled her in, and swallowed her.

<u>treacherous</u> (TRECH-er-us) dangerous

■ Talk About the Story

1. Why did the girl in the story need to find the Bird of Seven Colors?

2. Who else needed help from the Bird of Seven Colors? What kind of help did each need?

3. How did the girl get the information and help she needed from the Bird of Seven Colors?

4. What reward did the girl receive by helping the King's daughters and the mango tree? Did they learn the answers to their questions? How do you know?

5. What happened to the girl's mother? Why?

6. Do you think the girl's mother got what she deserved? Why or why not?

7. How might the story be different if the trick had not worked and the bird had discovered the girl?

■ Think About the Story

1. Describe the Bird of Seven Colors in your own words. Then draw a picture of what you think it looks like.

2. Why do you think the Bird of Seven Colors' mother decided to help the girl?

3. Do you think the girl would have shared the treasures with her mother? Why or why not?

■ Write About the Story

Imagine that you had met the girl on her way to find this Bird of Seven Colors. What question would you have wanted her to ask for you? How do you think the bird would answer? Explain your ideas in a paragraph.

At The Library

The trick to enjoying what you read is reading what you enjoy. If you liked the folktales in this unit, look for these books in your school library.

1. ***Alexandra the Rock-Eater,*** by Dorothy Van Voerkom. Published by Alfred A. Knopf in 1978.

2. ***Ramona Quimby, Age 8,*** by Beverly Cleary. Published by William Morrow & Co. in 1979.

3. ***Safiri the Singer,*** by Eleanor Heady. Published by the Follett Publishing Company in 1972.

4. ***The Three Wishes: A Collection of Puerto Rican Folktales,*** by Ricardo Alegria. Published by Harcourt, Brace Jovanovich in 1969.

Friendship

What does friendship have to do with cats?
Or sneezes?
Or hens?
How might friendship involve a grandma?

You'll find out as you read about the friends
and the friendships in this unit. You might
even make a friend or two of your own!

Keep a Poem in Your Pocket

by Beatrice Schenk de Regniers

Keep a poem in your pocket
And a picture in your head
And you'll never feel lonely
At night when you're in bed.

The little poem will sing to you
The little picture bring to you
A dozen dreams to dance to you
At night when you're in bed.
So—
Keep a picture in your pocket
And a poem in your head
And you'll never feel lonely
At night when you're in bed.

*How might a poem
be like a friend?*

Enjoying Poetry

Poems are special. They are a special way of sharing ideas, or feelings, or experiences. They are a special kind of writing. Because there are so few words in a poem, each word is chosen carefully. Perhaps it is the way the word sounds. Or the picture it paints. Or, the beauty of the word itself. Together, the words in a poem help us think about things in a way we might not have before.

In many poems, the lines end with a rhyming word. See if you can find the rhyming words in the poem on page 128.

As you read the following poems, think about what feelings or ideas each poet is trying to share.

School is Over

by KATE GREENAWAY

School is over!
Oh, what fun!
Lessons finished,
Play begun.

Who'll run fastest,
You or I?
Who'll laugh loudest?
Let us try.

*Which word tells about the feeling
of this poem: Sad, Happy, Fearful*

Poem

by LANGSTON HUGHES

I loved my friend.
He went away from me.
There's nothing more to say.
The poem ends,
Soft as it began—
I loved my friend.

*How do you think the poet feels about his friend's
leaving?*

131

Spotlight on

Langston Hughes

Langston Hughes had never thought of himself as a writer. He had never tried to write—not a single story, not even a poem. Then, one day, he was elected class poet.

"I guess I looked more like a poet than the other kids," he said. Well, Langston Hughes couldn't be class poet without writing a poem. So he did. He wrote a long poem about his school. He read the poem at graduation. His classmates and teachers loved it.

For Langston Hughes that graduation day was the beginning. Never again would he wonder about what to do when he grew up.

Other Books by Langston Hughes
Don't Turn Your Back: Poems
First Book of Jazz
First Book of the West Indies
Popa and Fifina: Children of Haiti
The Dream Keeper and Other Poems

CATS

by ELEANOR FARJEON

Cats sleep
  Anywhere
    Any table,
      Any chair,
        Top of piano,
      Window-ledge,
    In the middle,
  On the edge,
Open drawer,
Empty shoe,
  ANYBODY'S
    Lap will do,
      Fitted in a
        cardboard box,
      In the cupboard
    With your frocks—
  ANYWHERE!
    They don't care!
  Cats sleep—Anywhere

Where have you seen cats sleep?

---

cupboard (cuh-BORD) closet
frocks (FROKS) clothes

Understanding Shape Poetry

■ Reading About Shape in Poetry

You know that poets use words to share their ideas in a special way. Some poets also use shape. They write so that the words of a poem form a special shape. The shape has something to do with what the poem is about. It adds to the meaning of the poem.

Look back at Eleanor Farjeon's poem, "Cats." Decide how the shape of the poem helped add meaning to the poem.

■ Thinking About Shape in Poetry

Below is a shape poem by Marjorie Slavick Frank. Read the poem. Be ready to explain how the shape adds meaning to the poem.

Pogoing
by Marjorie Slavick Frank

pogoing from here to there

is thrice the distance anywhere

pogoing is slow goingoingoingoing

The Little Rain

by JUDITH THURMAN

the little rain
writes its name
in the dust:
on hoods of cars.
on window panes.
The BIG rain
comes with a
s w o o s h:
    cars
        panes
            dust
                names
        w h o o s h !

How does rain write its name?

135

Skinned Knee

by JUDITH THURMAN

My knee
knits itself
with in-and-out
stitches,

a rough patch
that itches-
but don't scratch!

There's skin
below,
still soft,
still
whole.
GROWING
 OWING
  WING
   ING
    N
    G

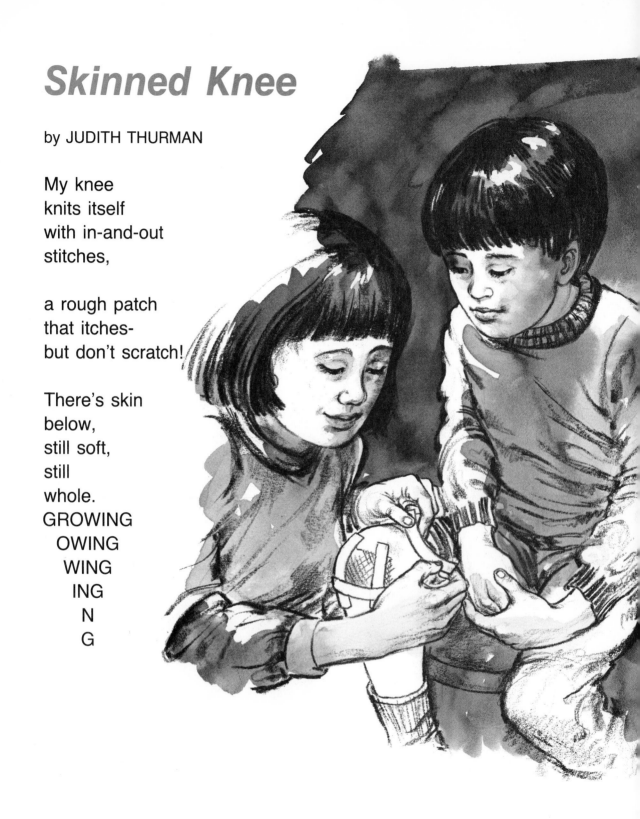

How do you keep yourself from scratching a skinned knee?

In "STAND BACK," SAID THE ELEPHANT, "I'M GOING TO SNEEZE!", an elephant tries to keep its friends from having a problem.

"Stand Back," Said the Elephant, "I'm Going to Sneeze!"

by PATRICIA THOMAS

"Stand back," said the elephant, "I'm going to sneeze! I hate to <u>alarm</u> you, but I don't wish to harm you. My friends, I fear it's clear. . . Oh, dear, You'd better stand back, I'm going to sneeze."

"Oh no, oh no!" cried the buffalo. "You're so big and strong and your trunk is so long, your sneezes send everyone flying along, bumping and thumping down pathway and trail, bounding and jouncing head over tail, tumbling and bumbling. Your sneeze is a <u>gale</u>. Or a hurricane! I hate to complain, but please, don't sneeze!"

"No, no, please, don't sneeze," cried the monkeys in the trees. "You make such a breeze when you sneeze. The last time you

---

<u>alarm</u> (a-LARM) frighten
<u>gale</u> (GAYL) strong wind

blew us right out of the trees. The branches began to bend and to sway and some of us landed so far away we didn't get back until the next day.

"The leaves all went whirling and tumbling and swirling, and the flowers shook for hours the last time you sneezed. Even a cough would knock some of us off. Oh, *please,* don't sneeze!"

With a shriek the parrot opened his beak. "The elephant says he's going to sneeze!"

"Oh, Elephant, please!" cried the birds in the trees. "The last time you sneezed we lost every feather. We didn't know whether we'd ever get back together. Every parakeet was bare as a sheet from his head to his feet. What's more, all the whales had peacock's tails, and the wings of the cockatoo were stuck on the kangaroo. You must <u>confess</u> it was quite a mess, very confusing and not too amusing. Even a snuffle makes our feathers ruffle. Oh, *please,* Don't sneeze!"

"Fly, fly," called the birds to the bees. "The elephant says he's going to sneeze!"

"Oh, no," buzzed the bees. "Not a sneeze! Not a sneeze! The last time he blew off our stings and our wings and we had to make do with rose thorns and glue. Furthermore . . . what a shock . . . we all had to walk . . . on our knees, if you please, (And that's hard on bee's knees) while our wings grew back in.

---

confess (con-FES) admit

What a sin! Oh, *please,* Don't sneeze!"

"Beware, beware," called the bees to the bear. "The elephant says he's going to sneeze."

"Oh, please, not a sneeze," said the bear. "That's not fair. I declare, the last time he sneezed he blew off all my hair, and left me so bare I spent the whole winter in long underwear—nothing's so sad as a bear that is bare. The poor giraffe (Don't laugh) almost bent in half, and the alligator's snout was turned inside out. The last time he sneezed. A sniff or a snuff is bad enough . . . But a sneeze! Oh, *please,* Don't sneeze!"

"I don't suppose you could hold your nose, or wait awhile?" asked the crocodile with a sad little smile.

"Oh my, do try," said the fly.

"We wish," said the fish, "you would if you could. The last time you blew off all of our scales from our heads to our tails, and our gills got the chills our skin is so thin. If you do it again we'll freeze! Oh, *please,* don't sneeze!"

The zebra yelled, "Yipes, you'll blow off my stripes, plus lots and lots of the leopard's spots, and all of the snakes will be tied up in knots!"

The hippopotamus said, "A lot of us will fall right on our bottom-us if you sneeze. So *please,* Don't sneeze."

"I'm sorry, my friends," said the elephant sadly. "About all of this I do feel badly. If I could keep from sneezing I'd do it gladly. But I have such a twitch in my trunk, and an itch, plus a bit of a tickle, and even a prickle. You must run, fly, and hop. I'm afraid I can't stop. I would if I could, but there's nothing to do . . . Ah . . . Ah . . . "

"BOO!" shouted a little gray mouse jumping out of his house. He stood right up on his little tiptoes, stuck out his tongue, and wiggled his nose.

"Eek!" shouted the elephant, jumping up in the air. "That's a mouse! That's a mouse standing there! I must hide in a tree before he gets me or jump in the lake. For goodness sake! Don't scare me! Please spare me!"

The mouse laughed, "Oh, pooh! Now what could I do? A little thing like me to a big thing like you? I only wanted to give you a scare, and it worked as sure as you're standing there. Elephant, think about it, please! You completely forgot to sneeze!"

"Well, what do you know?" laughed the elephant. "That's so! It's astounding, confounding. As I live and breathe! I don't think I really have to sneeze."

astounding (ah-STOUND-ing) surprising

confounding (con-FOUND-ing) confusing; hard to understand

140

He began to giggle. "He, he, he, he! That's the funniest thing that has happened to me! Ha, ha, ha! Ho, ho, ho!" The elephant shook from his head to his toe. He ho-hoed and ha-haed. He giggled and guffawed. He chortled and chuckled until his knees buckled.

He sat down and rolled from side to side. In fact, the elephant laughed till he cried. He laughed till the ground was shivering and shaking and all of the trees were quivering and quaking. The monkeys came tumbling out of the trees, and the stings fell off every one of the bees. The bird's feathers went flying to goodness-knows-where, and all of the hair fell off of the bear.

The giraffe bent in half, and the alligator's snout turned inside out. The fish lost their scales from their heads to their tails. The zebra yelled, "Yipes! There go my stripes!" While the hippo went thump right on his plump . . . you-know-what! And into a puddle the mouse went . . . ker-plop! Then he sat up and shouted, "This simply must stop! We're terribly glad you don't have to sneeze, but if you must laugh, laugh softly. Oh, Elephant, *please!*"

■ Talk About the Story

1. What problem did the animals have?

2. How did the animals try to solve their problem?

3. Why did the elephant's friends have a problem even though the elephant didn't sneeze?

4. Why do you think the elephant bothered to warn the other animals about the sneeze?

5. What do you think would happen to you if you were near the elephant at the time of a sneeze?

■ Think About the Story

1. If this story were a shape poem, what do you think it would look like?

2. How would the story have been different if it had been the mouse that was going to sneeze?

3. If the elephant had to sneeze, it probably means it had a cold. Where do you think an elephant could catch a cold?

■ Write About the Story

Think up some ways to help stop a sneeze. Be silly if you wish. Write your advice for sneeze-stopping as a poem. Make sure your poem tells a story too.

When the elephant spoke, his friends believed him. In "Santiago," things are different. Santiago must find a way to prove something to his friends, especially to Ernie. The problem is that the proof is a thousand miles away.

SANTIAGO

by PURA BELPRÉ

"Santiago!" Mother called from the kitchen. No answer. "Santiago Román!" Still no answer. His mother walked into the parlor. There sat Santiago staring at the light through the stereoscope.

"I have been calling you, Santiago. Did you not hear me?"

"But I am looking at the picture of Selina Grandmother sent me."

"Selina, Selina. Morning, noon and night, you speak of nothing else. You left her in Puerto Rico, but to hear you talk one would think she is here in New York. Put away that stereoscope. Come, have your breakfast or you will be late for school."

parlor (PAR-lur) a room in a home where visitors are entertained

143

Santiago gave the picture one more quick look, then put the stereoscope on the table next to a large carved gourd. Slowly, he followed his mother to the kitchen.

"May I take the stereoscope to school, Mama?"

"Whatever gave you that idea? You know we don't allow it out of the house."

"I want the children to see Selina too."

"So you talk about that hen at school also. Finish your breakfast, Santiago, before you have more silly ideas."

Santiago's mother handed him a paper bag. "Here's your lunch. The permission slip is signed. It is a good day to eat lunch by the river," she smiled. But Santiago ate only a little breakfast. Then he picked up his lunch and the slip and waited for his mother to get her pocket book.

How he wished he could take the stereoscope to school and show Selina to Ernie—especially to Ernie. Of the eight children in his class, Ernie was the only one who didn't really believe Selina existed. He wanted Ernie to believe about Selina.

"Let us go," said his mother.

The school was a block away, just around the corner from where they lived. They hurried to the corner, then had to wait for a green light before crossing.

"I don't see any other children going to school, Santiago. You must be quite late." The light changed and they rushed across. "Now run," his mother said and kissed him.

Santiago ran toward the main entrance. Halfway there he suddenly stopped. Was he seeing things? He closed his eyes and opened them quickly. It was true. Across the street and under a large log outside the parking lot, a hen—a large white hen—was pecking. Santiago ran on to the school. He *was* late.

When he entered his classroom, everybody was busy. "Listen everyone! I just saw a hen—a large white hen!" he cried.

Clay modeling, finger painting, block and cardboard building, raffia weaving, all stopped at once. All of the students surrounded Santiago—all but one. Ernie, whose hands clutched tiny nails and a hammer, paid no attention.

"Where did you see a hen?" asked the children.

"Nowhere. He did not see a hen," said Ernie without looking around.

"I did so," Santiago insisted.

"Here we go again," said Miss Taylor. "I feel just like a <u>referee</u>, and always the subject is hens. Let Santiago finish his story, Ernie."

<u>referee</u> (ref-uh-REE) someone who makes sure that game players follow the rules of the game

"You know the parking lot across the street?" continued Santiago. "Well, right there outside the wire fence is a large log. Pecking under the log is the hen."

"Oh, you only thought you saw a hen," said Ernie. "This is New York City. Hens don't walk in the streets here."

"This one does, because I just saw her."

"That's enough, Ernie," said Miss Taylor. "Santiago, you are sure you saw this hen?"

"Yes, Miss Taylor."

"Good. Then we can settle this matter. We will go and look at this hen."

"Now, now?" asked the children.

"Now we go back to work. On our way to the river, we will stop by the parking lot."

Work resumed. Lucille and Maria went back to their finger painting. Hector and Ernie began fixing the cardboard moat for their castle. Shirley and Clarice started sorting the seashells that were to be pasted on a sewing box. Santiago and Joseph began to cut table mats.

Miss Taylor gathered the raffia work and set it on a table close to her desk. She smiled to herself as she thought that for once the children were all working diligently. That Santiago, she thought, he seems to be in two places at once. He lives in New York, but his mind is full of his adventures with that pet hen back in Puerto Rico. Many times he has told the children

---

resumed (ree-ZOOMD) started again

moat (MOHT) a deep, wide ditch that is often filled with water

diligently (DIL-uh-jently) with much effort

about her. And all believe him, that is, all except
Ernie. You have to show Ernie.

"There's no more paste, Miss Taylor," said Clarice.
"Shall I get more?"

Miss Taylor looked at the clock. "If we are to stop
by the parking lot, we had better start getting ready.
Put everything aside and wash your hands."

Lucille and Maria were the first ones at the
washing sink. "I don't want a lick and a promise on
those hands. Wash them clean." All the children
washed and scrubbed as best they could. Soon they
were ready to go.

"Stay close to your partners," said Miss Taylor, and
led the way. They went down into the subway station
close to the school and out the opposite exit to save
time. Once outside, they went past the newspaper
stand, the drug store and the Elk's hall. Ahead was

the parking lot. Two workers in overalls were sitting on the log eating their lunches. The children surrounded them.

"Where is she?" asked Santiago.

"Where is who?" asked the men.

"The white hen," explained Santiago.

"Look, Sonny, this is a parking lot, not a chicken coop."

"See!" exclaimed Ernie. "I told you. You did not see a hen."

"Perhaps she is in the parking lot," suggested Santiago.

So they all peered through the wire fence, and they all saw cars and trucks of all sizes and colors, three large trees in the rear and a large bulldog tied to a post. But none saw a large white hen. While they were looking, another worker joined the two on the log.

"What goes on here?" he asked.

"A search for a hen. You did not see her, did you?"

"Who me? Is this a joke?"

"Let me explain," said Miss Taylor. "Come here, Santiago. This boy claims that he saw a large white hen pecking under this log this morning. We have come here in order to see her and to settle an argument. But if you, who work here, haven't seen a hen . . ."

"Wait a minute, lady," interrupted one of the workers.

"We did not say that we work here. The fact is, we work down the street and come here just to eat our lunch."

"I know someone who works here," said another.

"Wait just a second." He went to the corner shop and returned with a <u>stout</u> man dressed in blue overalls.

"This is Angelo. Tell him your story, boy." Santiago repeated the story once more. "Did you see her, Señor Angelo?" Angelo laughed. "Sure, sure," he said, still laughing. "That was my Rosina."

"But where . . ." Santiago didn't finish his question, for just then, through a hole in the wire fence, a large white hen appeared.

"Look, Ernie," he cried. "There she is! There she is!" Santiago jumped up and down.

"Stand still," said Angelo. "Don't frighten her. Let her come to me."

Everybody stood quietly. Ernie stared and stared. Slowly, like a <u>prima donna</u> on a great stage, Rosina walked straight to Angelo. He picked her up and smoothed her feathers.

"Does she live here?" asked the children.

"No, no. She lives just across from the George Washington Bridge. Everyday I bring Bravo, my bull dog, to guard the parking lot. Rosina stays at home. But she likes Bravo and misses him. So, every now and then, I bring her to be with him. Let us go and feed Bravo, eh Rosina?" He walked into the parking lot. Bravo saw them coming and his stumpy tail quivered in greeting.

<u>stout</u> (STOUT) fat

<u>prima donna</u> (PREEHM-uh DAN-uh) the most important performer

"Boy, that's a hen to beat all hens," said Ernie.

"All, except my Selina," said Santiago quickly.

"Oh, you just say so," said Ernie.

"I can prove it."

"How?" Ernie wanted to know.

Santiago did not answer. Instead he turned to Miss Taylor. "Please come to my home for a little while. It is just down the street. I want everyone to see my Selina."

"Your Selina? I thought she was in Puerto Rico." Miss Taylor was puzzled.

"When did she fly in from Puerto Rico?" taunted Ernie. Santiago ignored him. "Please, Miss Taylor," he pleaded.

"Well, it is irregular," she said. But something in Santiago's voice made her reconsider.

taunted (TAWNT-id) teased

irregular (ih-REG-yoo-lur) not usual

150

Was there something else besides Selina on Santiago's mind? Important as she was to him, was it Selina that really mattered now?

"All right, let us go," she said.

Santiago led the way to his home and rang the bell. His mother had never seen so many children in her home before. But if she was upset, Santiago certainly was not. Calmly he said, "This is my mother, Señora Roman. My father is not here. He is working." Then he turned to his mother. "Mama, they have come to look at Selina."

Everyone stood waiting for a hen to appear. Santiago took the stereoscope from the table and looked through to be sure the picture was straight.

"Now you all can see my Selina. Here she is!"

"How can she be in there? What is that?" asked Ernie ahead of everyone. Ernie always asked things first.

"A stereoscope," answered Santiago.

"A stereo what?" asked Ernie.

"Oh, something you use to look at the pictures."

"Moving pictures?" asked the children.

"No, just pictures, like the one there now."

"Let me see! Let me see!" cried the children.

Miss Taylor clapped her hands. "You are not in a playground. This is Santiago's home. We are his guests. Let us act accordingly."

"Oh, it's all right," said Santiago's mother.

"Only one person can look at the stereoscope at a time," said Miss Taylor. "Make a line."

Santiago passed the stereoscope to Lucille who was first. "I can see her from her crest to her legs. She is so colorful."

"Don't take all day. It's my turn now," said Horace. Lucille passed him the stereoscope.

"My, what a hen!" he cried. "All the colors of a rainbow."

And so the stereoscope was passed from hand to hand until it got to Ernie at the end of the line. Santiago held his breath. What would Ernie say? Santiago's face showed his anxiety and worry. Miss Taylor noticed him. So this is what she had sensed. Ernie. She should have guessed. This was the real reason for their visit. All of a sudden, she too became worried about what Ernie would say.

Ernie fixed the stereoscope to his eyes. He looked quietly for a while. He moved the stereoscope ever so slowly, back and forth. "Boy, this is the queen of all queens. When you move the stereo—stereoscope slowly, the hen seems to be moving. Gee, Santiago, I wish she was really here. We could put her in the

parking lot with Rosina. Say, 'Rosina' and 'Selina.' Their names sound alike."

Everybody laughed. But no one laughed more than Santiago. Gone were his anxiety and worry.

"Now that you have passed judgement on Selina," said Miss Taylor, "what about me? I too would like to see her." Slowly, Ernie passed her the stereoscope. She took one look. "Why, she is elegant!" she exclaimed. "You are right, Ernie, she is a queen. If I had a pet hen like this, Santiago, no one could keep me from talking about her."

Santiago beamed. Miss Taylor put the stereoscope on the table. It was then that she noticed the large carved gourd. "This is a work of art," she said almost to herself. But Santiago's mother heard her and joined her at the table.

"It's very old. Like the stereoscope, it has been in our family for a long time. It was carved by my grandfather, and it shows events in the history of Puerto Rico. See, here are the Indians, Columbus, Ponce de Leon."

The children surrounded her. "Turn it slowly, and tell more about it, like you tell me, Mama" said Santiago. So she did, and went on, absorbed in her telling.

"It is like hearing a book read aloud," said Miss Taylor when she had finished. She understood now why Santiago lived in two places at once.

"We must go, Señora Roman. This has been a day of surprises. I do want to thank you for your hospitality. It was generous of Santiago to invite us here."

"Our house is your house, but it is a fine day for eating lunch by the river. Enjoy it." Santiago's mother opened the door and the children filed out.

"Gracias! Thank you!" they chorused.

Once outside, they crossed the street and went skipping past the Hispanic Museum. Ahead, lunch bags swinging, feet marching to the beat of a mutual whistling tune, went Santiago and Ernie. On down the long block they marched, on and on towards Riverside Drive and the Hudson River.

Yes, it was a very fine day indeed for eating with one's friends by the river.

---

hospitality (has-pih-TAL-ih-tee) friendly treatment of guests
mutual (MYOO-choo-ul) shared

■ Talk About the Story

1. What did Santiago want to prove to Ernie and the other children in his class?
2. Why did Santiago have a problem proving his claim?
3. How did Miss Taylor help Santiago solve his problem?
4. Where does this story take place?
5. What other place is important in the story?
6. Why do you think it was so important to Santiago that Ernie believe him?
7. What did Santiago and Ernie do at the end of the story that showed they were friends?

■ Think About the Story

1. How would the story be different if it was told from Miss Taylor's point of view?
2. Suppose Ernie still did not believe that Selina was Santiago's hen, even after seeing the picture. What would Santiago do then?
3. Use your own words to describe Miss Taylor.

■ Write About the Story

If he could have, Santiago probably would have brought Selina to New York with him. Imagine that you are moving to a different part of the world. You can bring one thing from home with you. What would you choose? Why would you choose it? Explain your ideas in a paragraph.

Santiago worked hard to make Ernie his friend. "Kevin's Grandma" is a story of two boys who are already friends, and their very different grandmas.

Kevin's Grandma

by BARBARA WILLIAMS

I tell Kevin about my grandma. When I am sick she comes to see me in her blue station wagon. She brings presents like crayons and coloring books and ice cream.

Then Kevin tells me about his grandma. When Kevin is sick she brings him things like comics and homemade peanut-butter soup. She brings them on her motorcycle.

I like to sleep at my grandma's house when my parents go out of town. We play checkers and drink root beer. Sometimes we stay up as late as ten-thirty.

Kevin likes to sleep at his grandma's house too. They arm-wrestle and do yoga exercises. Then they send out for pizza at midnight.

Sometimes I help my grandma work. We put on white aprons to shell peas or make caramel popcorn balls.

Sometimes Kevin helps his grandma work. They put on bib overalls to fix her motorcycle chain. Or they hammer the shingles on her roof.

I take piano lessons from my grandma.

After each recital she takes all the kids out for ice cream.

Kevin takes judo lessons from his grandma. Afterwards they go to the health-food bar and drink tiger's milk.

My grandma belongs to a bridge club. She also belongs to a garden club and a music club. Last winter her music club put on a program for the children in the hospital.

Kevin's grandma belongs to a karate club. She also belongs to a scuba-diver's club and a mountain-climbing club. Last winter her mountain-climbing club spent two weeks on the top of the Grand Tetons.

On my birthday my grandma takes me out to lunch. Then we go shopping. She buys me any toy I want.

On Kevin's birthday his grandma takes him in an airplane. He watches from the window while she goes skydiving.

My grandma has a scrapbook showing all the things she used to do. She was the star of her high-school play.

Kevin's grandma used to work in a circus. She has a scrapbook with pictures showing how she could ride a unicycle on a tightrope. One picture shows her swinging from a trapeze by her teeth. Another picture shows her putting her head in a lion's mouth.

Once my grandma took me on a trip to Florida. We went in her blue station wagon and stopped overnight in a motel.

Once Kevin's grandma took him on a trip to California. They rode in twenty-seven different cars and trucks. They slept in haystacks and barns. And they even slept in a floating all-night monster movie in the middle of Lake Tahoe.

I'm not sure I believe everything about Kevin's grandma. Whoever heard of peanut-butter soup?

■ Talk About the Story

1. The story is about two grandmas. How are the grandmas different from each other?
2. How are the two grandmas alike?
3. Which grandma would you like to have? Why?
4. Do you think Kevin was telling the truth about his grandma or was he bragging?

■ Think About the Story

1. If the story is about two grandmas, why is it called "Kevin's Grandma?"
2. Describe Kevin's grandma's house in your own words.
3. How would the story be different if told by Kevin?
4. Do you think the storyteller wished he had Kevin's grandma? Why or why not?

■ Write About the Story

Think about an especially interesting person you know. In a paragraph tell why that person is interesting. Be sure to give an example.

At the Library

If you would like to meet more new friends like those you read about in this unit, look for these books in your school library.

1. **Eddie's Menagerie,** by Carolyn Haywood. Published by William Morrow & Co. in 1978.

2. **Kevin's Grandma,** by Barbara Williams. Published by E.P. Dutton in 1975.

3. **Santiago,** by Pura Belpré. Published by Frederick Warne & Co. in 1969.

4. **"Stand Back," Said the Elephant, "I'm Going to Sneeze",** by Patricia Thomas. Published by Lothrop, Lee & Shepard in 1971.